I0843444

OVERCOME FRENEMIES
How People Hold Us Down

Karen Kellock Ph.D.

Manual for
Superior Men

This is a complete theory based on Einstein physics, Political Psychology, Systems Theory and Archetypal Psychiatry.

FORMULA

**All success attraction
All disease obstruction
All recovery elimination**

You must fast on all three

OBSTRUCTIONS:

**People
Habit
Food**

OVERCOME FRENEMIES

Because women fight thru flying monkeys it's all about that--you face their *army*. She's the most dangerous person you ever knew, angering her army so cruel.   Feeling powerless the female seeks sidekicks and these can be very dangerous as she directs their hits.   The weak sadistic husband will sense who's jealous of her and nurture that contact for a future project. They play cute/clever games that destroy you and it comes from their friends.

FEELING A MISFIT

BEING UNWANTED AS A BABY

Being unwanted as a baby was the reason why you let the hobosexual into your home: to belong.

Needing to fit in but never really feeling like you do is a prison. Getting rid of this trend is **HEAVEN**.

We all have a strong drive to attach, to belong, to find our tribe but this easily becomes a prison, aye.

Some feel like they don't belong tho' they do everything right not wrong: in dress, speech or song.

They conform on the outside but inside they always feel like an outsider. It makes a sad gut, a depressor.

The harder they try to fit in the worse things get and they feel it in the gut, seeking addictive ruts.

They spin and spin in the same cycle: trying to fit more and more, feeling ill-fitting and abhorred.

They feel self-conscious and want to avoid social occasions. It's all dull and boring to them.

SURVIVAL THROUGH ATTACHMENT

The only way the misfit can survive is to attach to one who loves them and meets their needs.

Fitting in with complex trauma [being unwanted]: the only way the infant survives is by attachment.

Parental attachment: validation, security, feeling accepted & understood, loved & cherished.

FEELING A MISFIT

To find that one person means you can finally relax and be authentic without social punishment.

To return that love parents have a ton of influence with the child and peers can't impose their style.

They don't have to fit the new group cuz they already fit in with the family group: peers are poop.

If one doesn't have family attachment, he will so want to attach that he will adapt, to his detriment.

THE ADULT IN COMPLEX TRAUMA

The adult caught in complex trauma from childhood will be DESPERATE to attach so he will maladapt.

Being betrayed will activate this sad desperation and soon he'll be adapting to lower companions.

Parents relate on superficial issues but not authentic ones: child feel shame "I'm not good enough".

He can't get love and acceptance for authenticity, only by conforming to the mindset of the family.

If he's authentic, they withhold love and judge him. The love is very conditional and he knows it.

He begins to connect superficially but never deeply. Their link is unsatisfying without authenticity.

Thus complex [subtle] trauma is taking place. Conforming without authenticity is not feeling safe.

They find new acceptance but only if they conform to THAT group and here we go again, poop.

The new group talks love like you're part of the family, a sister or brother but soon it's another bother.

FEELING A MISFIT

I felt like I didn't belong my whole life. When I married an understanding man my career took off, aye.

My two older sisters were liberals and judged me constantly. They were raging feminists see.

The whole extended family were liberal and in their presence, tho I tried to adapt, I was miserable.

THE CHURCHES CALLED "FAMILY"

I tried churches calling me "family" but soon conformity would rear up and they would soon judge me.

It's the underlying SHAME of the unwanted that carries over like this to any group, that's the scoop.

They said they had "one too many" about me. I grew up with a sickened stomach, ever feeling sadly.

I sought addictive devices to adapt and fell in with lower companions and all their ridiculous crap.

I found an understanding man and married him and my life healed from there, feeling safe: amen!

The unwanted child is DESPERATE to attach, meaning: seeking crutches or putting up with lechers.

The effects of family betrayal shocked me so bad I was like a dying infant clutching for survival: fact.

I don't know what I'd do if I lost him but I think I'd be ok from all the great things I've learned from him.

EFFECTS OF BEING BETRAYED

Betrayal brings grief & anger at first but then the emotions shut down and never go back on.

FEELING A MISFIT

Flashbacks & intrusive thoughts happen out of nowhere and days are interrupted by them: despair.

When trust is broken like that the bad memories keep coming for months and years: fact.

Deep confusion occurs on an existential level: like "why the hell am I even here?": it's from the devil.

The betrayed are distracted, unable to focus. Projects are left uncompleted; the kids are a circus.

Going thru the motions of life but not really there: zombie mode. Gone are the days when life just flowed.

INTRUSIVE THOUGHTS OF BETRAYAL

Intrusive thoughts of betrayal and encroachment last for years. 40 years later they can trigger fear.

Betrayal is an amputation of thought life, where painful memories trickle in for decades, aye.

"Just forget it now" his friends will always say. But it just doesn't work like that unfortunately.

The betrayed becomes a different person, having lost the love making him whole: affirmation.

He stops taking care of himself and his presence and appearance goes to hell: just an empty shell.

Having lost all approval and confirmation his thoughts return to the good ol' days of happy lovin'.

BEING DIFFERENT BRINGS CRITICISM

Anyone different brings criticism. This is one of the hardest things about living in a small town.

FEELING A MISFIT

Movies offer great relief from human society today. Even the worst horror shows are better ok.

Young men <50 judge, feel entitled, make demands and turn on you suddenly: I don't recommend.

10% leaders vs. 90% led. Those who think, act and judge independently vs. indifferent immaturity.

Every experience leaves an indelible mark & at the end of your journey CHARACTER is the result.

BEWARE OF HOBOSEXUALS MALE & FEMALE

I like my creature comforts and letting someone move in ruins the whole dynamic: no way friends.

I tried that before and I'll NEVER try it again but if a woman needs approval she'll do that and give in.

Don't let the hobosexual in or he'll be opening your frig and pouring himself a glass of wine the pig.

I didn't even know any better. I was so lonely and needed male approval even from that loser.

No one falls in love so quickly as a narcissist who needs a place to live. Tho' he flatters he's still a pig.

When they're in your place they're in a free hotel with free everything. Leave for work, you'll see.

50-50 JUST FEELS LIKE 90-10

If she lives with him he expects 50-50 split. But if he lives with her, 100% he expects her to pay it.

They have no access to nice things or neighborhoods without "falling in love" with you, understood?

FEELING A MISFIT

Never be someone's gateway to your lifestyle. That was the biggest mistake I ever made girl.

He's got to come to you with HIS lifestyle that you can put together. Give up fantasies, be clever.

DANGERS OF MARRYING HOBOSEXUALS

Some women marry their hobosexual then his name's on her house. They divorce and split it: ouch!

Many hobos are apartment-hunting on dating apps. If she doesn't have one they ignore the lass.

They don't have a job or are forever switching jobs. Let them move in and they stop looking the slobs.

The hobo has a habit of never being single. He's a dependent and you MUST see this girl.

They always have a sob story: bad luck follows them everywhere. It's a sure sign so you should beware.

They've invaded your personal space. You must set a boundary and make em leave and quickly ok.

I was in so need of approval I didn't even notice what was happening when the hobo was napping.

HOBOSEXUAL BETRAYALS

I know a girl who had a hobo for six years until she caught him having sex while she was at work.

No wonder men feel they're much smarter than women, getting emotionally entangled with vermin.

How do they worm their way in then take over and destroy? it's usually sex before they annoy.

FEELING A MISFIT

Once they find out you have money, a car, weed or a place to stay they start courting you ok.

Some will do anything to avoid homelessness except get a job. Be leery girl and just trust God.

Hobosexuals are really attracted to the good girls. Those with a big heart and do good work.

It's parasitic: they wanna distract you and suck what they can outa you. Don't be a sucker Sue.

THEY WILL DISAPPEAR SUDDENLY

They will disappear suddenly and if you're heavily invested in them your life will be over honey.

Never let someone stay there whose name is not on the lease. In these latter days it's on the increase.

Men should not move in with women lest she be the man while being sucked dry by vermin.

Let a man live with you & end crying. Evict your lover who's a tenant & has a key but not paying?

What better place to lay up than with a woman who wants to cater to him and have him around?

A man who wants to move in with you is a man who wants to take advantage of you [sex too].

It's dangerous trying to evict a grown man. A restraining order may be needed or violence is certain.

THEY LOOK FOR HEAVYWEIGHTS

They may look for heavyweights, chunky: insecure and chummy. They just want a warm bed honey.

FEELING A MISFIT

How they do it: If she goes to work in the morning and doesn't wake you up, then just never leave it.

When they wanna crash on your couch they'll become a squatter and later claim they're a tenant, ok?

When it stops being a boy-girl thing and then becomes an issue of legal tenancy you've had it see.

The hobosexual considers sexually servicing you "good" as their way of paying rent: what a hood.

The hobosexual dates you with the sole interest of having a place to stay: it's the crazy latter days.

SHE'S LUSH WITH RESOURCES

The fatter girl is lush with resources: her fridge is full, her bed is warm and her body's sensitive.

Mid-aged women are selling their homes to get rid of their boyfriend [tenant]: what a climate!

Always question anyone wanting to move into your home as you will carry the financial load.

Do NOT house a man for the new gold-diggers are not women as of old but men raiding your home.

The get comfortable so fast. They'll open up the fridge, pour themselves some wine then crash.

We women easily give up our time and resources to help one who'd never EVER do the same for us.

These hobosexuals will keep their appearance up, to pick up women to have a place to stay hon'.

When a man needs you they just can't love you. They need a car to drive or place to sleep Sue.

FEELING A MISFIT

Y'all let a predator in your home and didn't know it. He seems so nice and good lookin' you believed it.

THE PURE SURVIVAL OF USING

It's pure survival as they look for someone to use. You're a stepping stone and that's all you are Sue.

Their only "I do" is "I do choose to use you". This is not respect, they have nothing to give you Sue.

If the woman is fat she's no chance to get a man any other way and here's this looker in her hay.

It's a hypnotic trance and pure denial. It's not just her taking a chance it could surely end it all.

By using you it's not a partnership, they see you as a comer and when done treat you like shit.

BIRDS OF A FEATHER

Birds of a feather: when the lowest one will bring the highest one down to make it even hon'.

Had I known these things I woulda saved myself years of torment so I do hope you will listen up.

If he needs you he won't want you and if he wants you he won't need you, always think of that Sue.

You're in for a bad ride as water seeks its own level, and when he changes you're living with the devil.

He's sleeping in your bed for free and doesn't have time for work so will NEVER support you see.

While he sleeps on your couch he says he's loving on you but really he just needs your house.

FEELING A MISFIT

It's a latter day phenomena because men used to be independent with a job and an apartment.

When it's all over and you're in a ditch you'll ask "how did I not see these red flags?" and flinch.

Be safe and hobosexual-free this holiday season, when it's cold outside and they seek you for a reason.

If you're having sex you as a woman naturally think it's a relationship and you're surely blind to all of it.

MOVING IN WITH WARP SPEED

Moving at warp speed: on the first date he's ready to move in with you without paying a thing Sue.

He expects you to give him stuff just by living with you. It's open season with the frig in open view.

I know it's hard out there, a survival of the fittest but you surely don't wanna be a victim of the twits sis.

People invaded my personal space for years and I didn't even know why I was always angry/in tears.

This is a 21st century war and it has to do with INVASION: of boundaries while treated as a whore.

It has to do with DAUGHTERS without fathers to coach the on what a real man is vs. the bummers.

It has to do with daughters of mothers who ALSO let men for free, thinking it's a noble way to be.

I've been there/done that and am paying with severe PTSD for being a dumb brat attracting rats.

Our sympathy & empathy as women has been weaponized against us and it's blocked success.

FEELING A MISFIT

Don't fall for sob stories or be pressured out of guilt: for not giving enough or sharing your stuff.

DECADES OF SOCIAL CONDITIONING

Decades of social conditioning to be kind, considerate and a "good hostess" has made us blind sis.

Men take advantage of this socialization and the kindness of women who lack good direction.

Women give of their bodies too easily and so giving their homes up to men happens suddenly see.

Women are seen as fools and dumb because of our empathy and kindness, don't you see sis?

The kind are taken as HUGE TARGETS for the survivalists out there, so be wise and beware.

Conditioned to be kind welcome mats with decades of thinking like that made us fools to catch.

WE'RE NICE LITTLE COMMUNISTS

We're little communists, feeling guilty not to share our wealth with the less fortunate and any old nut.

I was like that, the talk of the town taking in anyone but it wasn't a saint image but a pathetic one.

Take my slogan: Home is All Where I Walk Tall. Take in a man and you'll surely & soon have lost it all.

Through their manipulations they bring nothing but stress and labor into our lives, so be done.

We have to be manipulated into taking on that stress. We must be coerced and pressured see sis?

FEELING A MISFIT

Women seeking affection and genuine devotion are TRICKED into this charade and destruction.

They are squatters in women's homes and it's a new system of dis-ease and a very sick one.

It's a tragic thing the new homelessness but us women can't afford to support them all sis.

You simply don't have the means to subsidize a grown man/adult who goes from house to house.

Women already make less w/ less opportunities but are expected to do more for homeless males see.

Don't take on the burden of housing one who is supposed to go to a men's shelter for help hon'.

TRICKED BY THE ENTITLED

We are TRICKED into taking on a nurturing and caretaking role when they never would girl.

They feel ENTITLED to a woman's help, care and resources while they'd never do it for us.

He cajoles her into a mothering role, acting like he's her child. It's their socialization to feel so entitled.

There are way too many men expecting to be given a free ride and to be taken care of by women.

Contribute to food kitchens but don't bring someone into your home to exploit & be a danger friend.

There is NO benefit for a woman to let a random man into her house. It will always cause pain, ouch.

They openly discuss with others how they tricked you into this so you should be disgusted sis.

FEELING A MISFIT

When he comes over he's just taking while not replenishing and you girl are just a lackey see.

Women improve men's lives with their order, intelligence and cleanliness but a man must afford this.

DENIAL OF THE HIGH COST OF GIVING

A woman usually won't see the high cost until her life is in shambles, a survivor of fake love lost.

The bums just drain the women they latch onto, not working on themselves in the interim too.

These are parasites who having drained one victim will promptly move on to the next, using sex.

AFTERTHOUGHTS

You learn things about yourself like: have almond butter first not after the meal or it's burp burp burp.

With Donald J. Trump all prices will start to plummet and groceries will no longer break your budget.

THE EFFECTS OF TRAUMA

SUBTLE TRAUMA: THE UNWANTED
ACCEPTING THINGS YOU SHOULDN'T
UNWANTED CHILDREN: "ONE TOO MANY"
RESULTS OF AN ANGRY MOTHER
ANXIETY AND ABANDONMENT
NO TOOLS TO REGULATE EMOTIONS
SHAME: I'M A LOSER TO BLAME
PESSIMISTIC AND SKEPTICAL
KEEPING BUSY TO NOT REMEMBER
EFFECTS OF BETRAYAL TRAUMA
HAUNTING LONELINESS: BETRAYAL
ONCE BETRAYED, IT'S HARD TO TRUST
HOBOSEXUALS WANT IN!
IF YOU ARE A CONSERVATIVE
FOUR DAY FAST ON "TAHINI BLEND"
THE INTESTINAL BROOM

THE EFFECTS OF TRAUMA

SUBTLE TRAUMA: THE UNWANTED

You've got BIG trauma then you have SUBTLE trauma appearing in less blatant but daily dramas.

Subtle trauma is a daily drone of low pitched pain, a brain fog of unhappiness each and every day.

Subtle trauma is like a big disappointment you've gotten used to as self-worth plummets to a boring stew.

You stop objecting to things you should object to, the things that anyone with self-worth would Sue.

The things self-worth would say "sexually harass me anymore and I'll call the sheriff" you're ok with.

ACCEPTING THINGS YOU SHOULDN'T

As you adapt to things you shouldn't, self-worth plunges more as their evil becomes dogged.

The "big 3" are neglect, abuse and abandonment. These create subtle trauma to one's detriment.

Betrayal, cultural, social and generational trauma can create this seething undercurrent of drama.

Were you a mistimed baby? This creates a subtle tone of unwanted carrying thru to your adulthood.

The sensitive child picks up they were unwanted, an afterthought, or "we had one too many" stuff.

UNWANTED CHILDREN: "ONE TOO MANY"

EFFECTS OF TRAUMA

Children of unwanted pregnancies are at risk for both behavioral and psychological issues too.

Such complex but subtle trauma results in maladaptations in adolescence creating drama.

The fetal autonomic nervous system is affected by maternal emotional adverse state: HATE.

RESULTS OF AN ANGRY MOTHER

If the mom is in negative emotional state it DOES affect the fetus and it all comes out in adolescence.

It angry mother affects the child later, in things like impeded social development: he's a nut.

Her anger activates the child's stress system in the womb and later in adulthood: a sense of doom.

When mom feels joy her body releases oxytocin and the child grows up happy and the favorite son.

Oxytocin is the "bonding hormone" so he grows up socially known with a happy life filled with fun.

There is no attachment/abandonment anxiety with a happy mom but he can't get along if an angry one.

ANXIETY AND ABANDONMENT

Things like anticipatory anxiety or partner abandonment affects fetus and later the woman/man.

If mom is stressed about the financial or anything else, that affects the child in utero or adolescence.

If a child is unwanted there will not be the attachment with parents nor later with anyone else.

EFFECTS OF TRAUMA

This "interrupt secure attachment" ends in a helluva life seen later in bad marriages filled with strife.

If parents get frustrated easily or lash out at the child he gets a complex or is filled with guile.

They meet physical needs but not the emotional ones of the child. Tho' "lucky" he has a neurotic style.

Without secure attachment or emotional needs there is lack of brain development or maturity see.

Sometimes it manifests in being angry, other times in being **TOO FRIENDLY:** all from attachment anxiety.

NO TOOLS TO REGULATE EMOTIONS

This child has no tools nor ability to regulate emotions so later is a nuisance or creates fire storms.

The mal-development of the brain and the emotions: that's the end result, being ornery and dumb.

The negative effects affects physiology too. The immune system or heart becomes a toxic stew.

An unwanted child may show an unconscious wish to die. Skeptical, pessimistic, mistrustful, aye.

Deep shame, suicidal ideation, can't believe they are loved: only solved by God's love from above.

Deep shame leads to a feeling of not fitting in or belonging. The unwanted feel is unrelenting.

SHAME: I'M A LOSER TO BLAME

Shame: they're a loser so everything must be their fault. Can't get over embarrassment of it all.

EFFECTS OF TRAUMA

DEEP insecurity and loneliness, a sense of impending doom and wanting to be away from all of this.

She needed the taste trip or other sensual delights. This led to obesity, anorexia or bulimia, aye.

PESSIMISTIC AND SKEPTICAL

Pessimistic and skeptical about everything in life. Life is a negative thing for them, it's only strife.

If unwanted, can't trust parents nor others later and this is the personality style of sisters/brothers.

What a life has accrued from pissed off mothers and absent fathers: an angry world in the gutter.

Unloved by parents, when one truly loves em they can't absorb or even discount/are annoyed by it.

Putting up with rough treatment was me, a masochist. It was a horrible life but I was used to it.

If undeveloped/an incomplete human, you're treated as subhuman and the results are armagedoom.

KEEPING BUSY TO NOT REMEMBER

I had to keep busy or I remembered too much. Like all of us I needed distractions for weeks & months.

After a life of this, I learned what I needed as a writer then God gave me a mansion with great favor.

Seeing the whole scheme I recalled what mom said when young: "it will all even out in the end hon'."

I try not to recall the crap and focus on the NOW when I've been incredibly blessed: wow.

EFFECTS OF TRAUMA

I even felt guilty for what I had now but then I recalled all I went through which was absolute hell.

Fighting em won't help since it was 30 years ago. Only forgiveness stops the acid reflux etc ya know.

EFFECTS OF BETRAYAL TRAUMA

When flattery and charm don't work they play victim to win your sympathy or some get violent see.

Betrayal is inevitable in these relationships so what are the everlasting feelings one gets from it?

The results of betrayal trauma are shock, denial and disbelief. It's abandonment and terror see.

Then you go into deep grief and sadness leading to hopelessness and complete emptiness.

Life feels so negative, painful and dark. This leads to anger & rage: irritability becomes your mark.

Fear, terror and paranoia: everything becomes scary. You're easily startled and annoyed early.

Next is guilt: I musta done something wrong, it's surely my fault. All these emotions form a quilt.

All this triggers core shame: see, I'm not lovable or valuable--creating more loneliness, that's all.

All this leads to NUMB: not feeling anything and being totally detached. Whole cultures get like that.

HAUNTING LONELINESS: BETRAYAL

The haunting loneliness after betrayal can be overwhelming, and this leads to the zombies.

EFFECTS OF TRAUMA

What's left after betrayal trauma is a deep feeling of being violated. It's a soul stabbing, mutilated.

Then comes emotional deregulation: from panic attacks to apathy, great difficulty staying even.

Massive mood swings in one day, or triggered from zero to a hundred in a frightening/dangerous display.

From panic to apathy: the things they used to enjoy don't do a thing for them now or they annoy.

Some go to suicidal ideation, for what's the point of living? Betrayal trauma just keeps on giving.

Then comes the cognitive symptoms of betrayal: flashbacks, nightmares and intrusive thoughts.

One is distracted and unable to concentrate. He seems disoriented and untrustworthy, a real flake.

What's the purpose of living? Who am I? Do I even matter? This is the confusion, a real bummer.

ONCE BETRAYED, IT'S HARD TO TRUST

Disassociation: complete detachment from life as if you're not really there. Forget life, it's just unfair.

One trusted but was then betrayed, so they lose confidence in any/all decisions they made.

Betrayal creates constant chatter in the brain. I'm not good enough, I'm horrible and life is rough.

The physical symptoms of betrayal mimic heroine detox: shaking, sweating, heart attacks.

Insomnia, constipation, joint pains, migraines. The body starts to crumble and you feel insane.

EFFECTS OF TRAUMA

Can't sit still or the whole gastrointestinal system is thrown off. Ones appearance looks rough.

Some get startled easily, some sleep all the time. Betrayal trauma varies but the cause is the same.

A common but tragic reaction to betrayal is promiscuity. This never works, making things worse quickly.

HOBOSEXUALS WANT IN!

Of course the hobo wants in your home. That's where everything is: your bounty, everything you own.

Warmth, cool comfort, all the goodies you accumulate, your great cooking: of COURSE he's coming.

Home is where it's all at and he wants in. He doesn't know how to create a home, its just bedlam.

Once I let him in, he'd get violent if I didn't let him in again. I had to relocate or face destruction.

It's as bad as any addiction: you give him a little booze and he'll beat you up for more: its HOME hon.

Living in a small liberal town without fences taught me all I needed to know about the leeches.

It was downright savage what the liberal commies put me through, always wanting what I have too.

I live in conservative America now where everyone minds their own business, staying home.

They were always dropping by and I thought I'd lose my mind along with being nervous all the time.

In my new area every moment is my own. I can be sure of precious privacy: it's like a heavenly home.

EFFECTS OF TRAUMA

IF YOU ARE A CONSERVATIVE

If you're a conservative you can't have anything more to do with liberal friends lest you argue with em.

The differences are just too great at this point: an historical breach that God won't anoint.

When I split from [blocked] old liberal friends I felt a release of energy and enormous bliss, amen.

The gap is too great now. Oil and water don't mix and you'll feel crazy with liberal friends around.

When I unfriended liberals I felt a fresh breeze, it was a balmy day and I was so very happy suddenly.

Liberal thinking is bad and very dishonest. Evil always calls itself "good", just as the bible says.

Liberals are getting completely different news--fake news and lies--so arguing is of no use.

If a friend parrots CNN saying "Trump's a dictator" you know it's a frenemy so just say "see you later".

It's come to this: if one watches Fox and another CNN there's no way of being friends with them.

ABC's the worst but the mainstream news are ALL BAD. We've never seen anything like this commie fad.

Harris and anyone else: If you wanna know what they plan to do, look what they did before this.

FOUR DAY FAST ON "TAHINI BLEND"

Try this for a 4-day fast: blend raisins, tahini, coconut flakes and almonds--eat a little/have a blast.

EFFECTS OF TRAUMA

This tahini blend [of fruit/nuts/seeds] is packed with antioxidants and you'll feel real good on it.

Every so often regular food blocks up. You don't feel good and gain weight: fast to get back up.

My tahini blend is a camouflaged fast and you'll be amazed how quickly you return to base.

Of course the maximum is a water fast but for most this does the detox job and you'll have a blast.

Raisins are a most alkalinizing fruit and along with coconut, almonds and tahini you'll be cute.

The highest nutrients are fruits, nuts and seeds. You're getting it in this blend which is superior see.

THE INTESTINAL BROOM

The raisins will maximally clean the intestines and you can feel it as it brooms out the toxins.

I hate when several days of eating blocks up. You need a hiatus: a two-speed life to get back up.

Digestion slows with stress. In these days of mess we tend to hold water and bloat up [lose finesse].

We need a change when this happens: give body a rest and thorough cleansing to rearrange atoms.

When your flesh jiggles, when your clothes don't fit right: these are signs to fast or go light.

With stress or even bad memories you'll retain water. As we age these tendencies worsen altogether.

The camouflaged fast reverses the matrix. Retained water goes out, you're again a cute chick.

EFFECTS OF TRAUMA

For something different on your partial fast, eat salsa on lettuce: this too is detoxing, as much as raisins.

I take a fruit/seeds/nuts/salsa/lettuce fast about ten days a month and view it as a trip [fun].

I get depressed when the scales go up for no reason. It's from water retention: time for fastin'.

The necessity of living a two-speed life is clear. Just like the weekdays vs. the wonderful weekend differs.

Caveat to all compulsive weighers: a dietary upgrade increases muscularity so you'll weigh more.

You'll look thinner but weigh more since muscles use less space but are heavier: you're lookin' niftier.

NARCISSIST SPIRIT

BOUNDARIES ARE ALL
IT'S A NO WIN SITUATION
TRAUMA DUMPING
INVADED BY A GANG OF BOYS
THE SEASON OF TREASON
YOU LET IN THE SNAKE
THE REPROBATE MIND
BE ROOTED IN GOD NOT "HIM"
AUTHENTICITY OR ATTACHMENT?
TRAUMA IS THE LOSS OF SELF
NEVER FORCE WHAT'S MEANT TO BE
HE MAKES THE MOLD FOR HER
SEE HIS SADISTIC PLEASURE
HEALTH PROBLEMS FROM NARC
GOING NO CONTACT WORKS
THE INSULT OF COMPARISON
PUSH PULL EFFECT
WHAT A COWBOY EATS
THE FALSE CHURCH

NARCISSIST SPIRIT

BOUNDARIES ARE ALL

I was too young to understand boundaries, trauma, boys and the necessity of living in a bubble.

Most in the United States are reprobate and that's why they can't see what you see about sin ok.

Protect your pets: from kids who didn't get what they wanted or the vindictive violence of exes.

The wounds transform us into something we are not. It took me decades to get back to self/God.

What you thought was "friendship" was Satanic opposition. Let God lead you from now on.

The mean comparisons are always there. You always feel minimized no matter how great you are.

IT'S A NO WIN SITUATION

There's no winning in this situation. He always has supply waiting on the side while you worsen.

Revelation: God wants you happy every day! It's hard to believe after the hell you've had to pay.

This is gonna make you warm steel and a velvet glove. You've overcome the worst but still can love.

Keep a journal, this is not your imagination. He's kept you up and down by pure sadistic intention.

Starving for affection and attention she was targeted by a narcissist who lovebombed and won.

NARCISSIST SPIRIT

They're out to get her, seeking to break her down. Better have boundaries or prepare to drown.

TRAUMA DUMPING

She tends to "trauma dump": inappropriately overshare her troubles with just about anyone.

She dumps her bad experiences without warning or invitation. It's an explosion and embarrassin'

After a psychic opening I returned to the beginning, feeling five again playing on the swings.

I was trauma dumping all the time, with anyone who'd listen about the terrible situation of mine.

INVADED BY A GANG OF BOYS

The boys had no lines, boundaries or morals and worst of all felt totally entitled and it was awful.

The cops wouldn't arrest em and once they knew it I felt totally trapped in a small desert town.

Liberals run in gangs--lunatic mobs the constitution calls it--roaming around looking for trouble.

They can't just stay home, they wanna come to your house bringing all their friends/lush & louse.

THE SEASON OF TREASON

It was my season of treason, my canyon on the hero's path, my Ph.D. in the streets, my facing Goliath.

They woke me up at midnight to fix them tacos, a great banquet for ten for all their friends.

Then after waking me up they told me how they wanted their tacos, like I was their slave ya' know.

NARCISSIST SPIRIT

It was all social after the greatest generation of meritocracy. EVERYTHING is social you see.

People will impose if you let em: while looking innocent they'll be roping you into boring obligation.

Relocation: the greatest high in life. Like being yanked out above the strife and put in new light.

From mob gang-ups & gossips you're surrounded by smiles and welcoming encouragements.

New home/area, laying new boundaries based on wisdom from what you went thru back then.

Strategic relocation: From ravenous wolves [ex friends] to a brand new start and maybe even loves.

It's as though demons control whole towns, regions, states, families, cliques, tribes and nations.

Just cuz the narcissist forges ahead doesn't mean he'll ever be successful due to dense mental.

Burning people outa their homes is an old tactic used to steal their lands and it's happening in Cans.

YOU LET IN THE SNAKE

If you let a snake in don't complain when you're bitten. It was YOU who brought this all on woman.

The reprobate porn-sick husband says "it doesn't mean anything to me" like that makes it ok see.

They can't see sin for what it is so never ask to be forgiven. Look around you, see it brethren.

COLLAGEN: the system works to restore skin, tissues and joints with restorative [deepest] sleep.

NARCISSIST SPIRIT

He was always at my front door, bothering me constantly just because I decided to be a loner.

The feeling of being invaded/overtaken by men--in groups--is forever etched in my worldview.

Women are just as bad given the chance. The Jezebel spirit given a leg up always takes advantage.

THE REPROBATE MIND

Reprobates can see truth then ignore it. What's obvious to you isn't to them, the anosognosic.

Anosognosia: the characteristic of all addictions as the victim can never see his own condition.

The reprobate can't see what's right in front of their face. Try to explain to him, it only frustrates.

There are no miracles with unbelief. It's sort of the key to directing your focus to the event to see.

The image is maintained to cover a lake of shame inside, always/forever suffocating the psyche.

It's cowboy country but full of polygamy. Big houses and silence, peaceful tranquility, order see.

BE ROOTED IN GOD NOT "HIM"

The stress of em in your life drives you mad but putting boundaries on em makes you feel bad.

Addiction: Relief in short term, negative consequences in long term and CANNOT give it up ever.

Ask him what he likes about you: it's always about how you're helping him never about you Sue.

NARCISSIST SPIRIT

If God put you together, chasing him is not only unnecessary but counterproductive see.

So take your eyes off of your desperate love object and back on yourself. People worship sux.

AUTHENTICITY OR ATTACHMENT?

We need two things: attachment and authenticity but that bond is threatened by me being me.

To stay attached we squelch our own authenticity every time and that's the problem friends of mine.

To stay attached we lose connection to our true selves and gut feelings. We stuff/drink em down see.

Authenticity threatens attachment even more in modern settings where we must conform see.

Once we give up essential authenticity we ask "who the hell am I and what's the point anyway?"

"You have to conform". "Who am I" was not even a question I asked, I just sought relief/warmth.

The magic healing happens with reconnection to that true self, unfelt since the childhood hell.

Trauma: Disconnection from self brings negative view of world/oneself and combative defense.

TRAUMA IS THE LOSS OF SELF

The loss of self is the essence of trauma. The purpose of all treatment should be reconnection.

Let go of what no longer serves you to make space for that which inspires you. Make a space Sue.

NARCISSIST SPIRIT

The associations of your past will drag you down and hold you back. Your whole history seems bad.

A sick relationship can damage your business, family and mental life. It's a demon from hell: strife.

Just as it's easy to accumulate belly fat, bad friends can be hard to get rid of too but we must, alas.

With relocation it may be not one will follow you in any way. It's as tho' it was a bad dream ok.

Not one person followed me. It was as tho' demons were just tied to that country, and I was free.

t was all just a lesson, my Ph.D. in the streets. I learned about people by encountering the mean see.

Mean old women when they had control, mean young jezebels calling you old, I experienced it all.

God put me through the ringer to teach this lecturer about people and not from books but pure evil.

It's the tribulation before triumph: wait patiently for victory while getting thru treachery.: look up.

NEVER FORCE WHAT'S MEANT TO BE

You never have to force anything that is truly meant to be. Wait on God and STOP chasing the "he".

God's purposes go deep. I prayed for the end of abuse and got thru it to now administer to you.

You can be in heaven before you die, just fly above the human race that thinks it's superior, aye.

He's gross and cruel, very social. That would scare any spiritually driven woman who's inner not low.

NARCISSIST SPIRIT

He constantly minimizes achievements [devil!] thru petty comparisons as if she's on their level.

Your achievements are constantly trivialized thru comparisons though many aren't even relevant.

You're not in the same league, you're totally unique--but the narc triangulates you see.

HE MAKES THE MOLD FOR HER

The narc transforms her into a mold that is acceptable to him yet he still finds flaws in her plans.

Nothing is ever enough cuz he's empty and projects that onto her. No wonder they're both sour.

He flatters for power. Handle this thusly: BELIEVE what he says about you but separate the deceiver.

He flatters for power--so you'll love him. Take his words as truth but see HIS manipulation.

He triangulates you with inferior others on inferior grounds and it's so insulting, so REBOUND!

Keep your focus on his grandiose phoniness, his lying, his triangulating and cruel manipulating.

SEE HIS SADISTIC PLEASURE

FOCUS on how he takes sadistic pleasure in punishing you. You've gotta get rid of this phony fool.

It is time to leave the relationship and never look back. His symptoms only worsen so forget that.

The perp is completely cut off from any insight or reflection so stop hoping & listening to him.

NARCISSIST SPIRIT

They're unaware of their instinctual responses or what they've done. Triggering jealousy for fun?

Blame-shifting and projection is how he rules his world and that's not gonna EVER change girl.

He must project his emptiness onto you and the only way it's done is to compare/pull you down too.

Do not waste any more time. Take the step and leave the relationship with a pit viper [snake like].

You have ailments you never had before. That's from a constant chemical cocktail living in a war.

You can't sleep, always anxious and panicking. These are the symptoms: leave and be happy.

Exposed to an abnormal amount of stress, you continue depleting just for your surviving.

Your body is not designed for war without R & R. Walking on eggshells was hell, I remember.

Your body is designed to relax in comfort cuz you happily live in a loving, nurturing environment.

HEALTH PROBLEMS FROM NARC

You don't get these health problems with a healthy partner. It's the STRESS, tantamount to war.

If you don't leave you'll turn into a shell you don't recognize. Then he'll attack you more, aye.

The mere fact he's successful in triggering reactions is proof you must leave: read above sections.

He treats everyone nice but you. Once you see the hypocrisy and mask-varying leave him Sue.

NARCISSIST SPIRIT

Notice his shape-shifting. Hit a roadblock and he becomes a completely different visage see.

For a narcissist your autonomy is a killer. They've lost control then and that's number one sir.

Say "Yep, I'm good" but don't ask about them. You've overshared in the past and it's embarrassin'.

If necessary he morphs into an entirely new human being: more than an actor, he's a magician.

If he makes your days sad or tormented that's all you need to break it off and finally be done with it.

Stop tormenting over all his facades, avatars and fake selves. You'll never reconcile it all you know.

You're giving him 100% of your attention while he has no time for you. Helluva situation Sue.

His attention is divided between 1000 fans yet each of them give him 100%: unfair deal man.

He has 1000 faces. Go beyond that to the evil spirit compelling him to kill, overtake and erase.

He's jealous of your success: imagine that. He aims to block it any way he can the dirty rat.

Injure a narcissist and he avenges a life of similar situations going back. It's deep/you're dead.

GOING NO CONTACT WORKS

Going no contact works. It gives you head space and clarity to work things thru/be happy now too.

No contact gives you rest from cortisol and adrenalin, your constant companions since this union.

NARCISSIST SPIRIT

No contact is based on this fact: they'll never change. Overcome this sad era and be a sage.

His antics to control you are so gross he always falls into his own net. Write em down/don't forget.

You don't want this behavior in your life. You want to get better and grow from this, free of strife.

It's time to leave if you can clearly see they are a narcissist. If they have all the signs, EXIT.

Never justify staying with him cuz he did one thing great. These are crumbs compared to hate.

Do NOT get myopic looking at individual instances. Look at the whole scene for it stinks sis.

Face the temporary pain of ending it vs. the never-ending pain of staying for he'll never change.

The PAIN OF STAYING will never get better. You can count on it only increasing: always remember.

Even if he makes you unhappy/triggers anxiety half the time it's too much don't you see Lassie?

It's unfair comparisons which piss you off the most. They're demeaning but expect it from the low.

He's a narcissist: incapable of change save a massive miracle on the inside from God above ok.

You gotta really see this guy: he'll always get bored, always discard and look for new supply.

Everything good from a relationship you'll never get from this man except in breadcrumbs.

THE INSULT OF COMPARISON

NARCISSIST SPIRIT

The whole thing was so insulting the way he compared you to a nothing but that's the devil: leveling.

He's texting all the time, that's how he keeps em all in line to assure he gets approval [shine].

Just remember: its the unfair comparisons that are the most controlling, humiliating and injuring.

Understand in your sad heart the symptoms and what you've been thru: coddle and nurture YOU.

Overcome him and you've graduated with a new degree. Understanding peeps, and free.

For it is toxic [unfree] to walk on eggshells. You know exactly what I mean by now, it was HELL.

He's not his many faces but the spirit behind. It means to kill, steal and destroy and is all about "I".

He's influenced by this, then that. Then he meets new supply and drops the prior in one minute flat.

He brags he's religious then caves into gross debauched worldliness like god Dionysus.

What if you caught him, how would you keep him? Your pain would be endless as years go on.

Narcissists are untrustworthy and dangerous. Especially after you escape, expect vengeance.

People were always pressuring me to do something. You gotta have a firm "NO!" to be queen.

PUSH PULL EFFECT

The push and pull effect within a toxic relationship produces a chemical cocktail of hardship.

NARCISSIST SPIRIT

This is about overstimulation of your nervous system. You need no-contact for rest/relaxation.

Trauma bonding only happens in toxic relationships with a push-pull effect with nerves wrecked.

You can't eat nor sleep, all you can do is think about them constantly. That's a trauma bond see.

You already know you gotta watch everything you say. You've already witnessed his raging ok.

You already know you can't say what you want around him, that you fear his sudden eruptions.

WHAT A COWBOY EATS

A cowboy eats a steak in the morning and is good to go for three days. That's how I like things ok.

A salad has no staying power, you want a steak to take you thru challenges and work for 36 hours.

A cowboy doesn't know where he'll end up or get the next meal. Only a steak or the like is ideal.

How much of being "multiply chemically sensitive" is actually from being protein deficient?

THE FALSE CHURCH

They prefer chanting to hearing God's condemnation of sin in the bible. That's too revealing of evil.

They want images/icons of God when the bible clearly forbids it. No bible, listen to the priest kid.

No chanting, no images, no icons or incense, no robes and rituals--what's left? Just the BIBLE.

NARCISSIST SPIRIT

It was a miracle, a magic coincidence. A straw house on my new property that gave me wellness.

EFFECTS OF BROKEN TRUST: NO MIRACLES

TRUST is like a fabric going thru every cell. BETRAYAL tears it all to hell--she feels like an empty shell.

If he's weak the man will destroy you cuz he's not strong enough to keep things away that will kill you.

BETRAYED WIFE TESTIMONY:
  Journey thru a Type One Trauma

I always felt it creeping in again--a wife knows thru symbols he's not all there anymore in his sin. I thought he was one person but the spirit he's into shows he's another--a demon from hell not my brother. I can never again withstand the smut of men and I'll stay alone in withering solitude till I meet a gentleman.

My lovely home, my starry reality, my life and wisdom was sullied--dirtied--by this horrible tragedy. Home life means everything to me. I banked on an illusion. I wanted peace and stability so bad I screened out reality as we both said "love ya, hon" I feel a tragic cry in my throat even as I'm writing this. Crying jags are common with the wife and kids.

I will study betrayal trauma and broken bonds for the rest of my days. The relief already is truly amazing. So let me get this straight: you miss me so much you gotta look at nude teens. I'm finally free of this lying!

COMMENT BY A BETRAYED WIFE

The other day he said he couldn't take the trash due to a bad back. I said OK. I came back ten minutes later and he was up and about, into his porn. All day long it's politics or porn. It's these little deceptions...and what was that blanket doing in his back seat? If he wanted it for the cold, why isn't it there now? LITTLE THINGS like that—from partial disclosure, enough to drive you wild—put us into our INVESTIGATIVE BEHAVIORS which become our new illness. God help us

LOST AND FATHERLESS

STAY HOME AND THRIVE
SINGLE IN A SHACK
A GENERATION OF LOST KIDS
SPEAK ABOUT YOUR PLIGHT
NEW TRENDS WITH YOUNG MEN
IRRATIONAL FEAR OF AGING
IT'S ABOUT LOYALTY NOT ATTRACTION
SPEAKING TOPICS OF SYSTEM REFUGEES
YOUR DESTINY IS THE HIGHEST
COMPLETION OF CREATIVE ACT
ELDER VISION: HOME IS GALAXY
TRUST HOW THE STORY ENDS

LOST AND FATHERLESS

If she didn't like what you said she'd ruin your rep. Smear campaigns of fake queens = death.

Stop exhausting disputes with frenemies. Just live in a separate stream see, a parallel society.

To adapt to a problem environment you either get sharper or the mind plays tricks more.

Be prepared for the gold ring to come around again. Practice, see yourself grabbing it and win.

You'll do yourself a world of good never to go there again. Now live a far happier life friend.

The bible says don't fret when wicked flourish like the green tree cuz they're cut down soon see.

STAY HOME AND THRIVE

Don't ever go back where angels fear to tread. He's hurt you before he'll do it again my friend.

I suppose I acted like that in the past for we swim in muddy waters and didn't know any better.

The pattern of narcissists is changing constantly sis: it's quicksand and hell for sensitives.

He loves you then someone else. This is not stability for rising talents need support to grow.

Don't get into cars with strangers and never let em into your house: warning from 1950's parents.

Trusting in/depending on man is like living on parched land/quicksand trying to get their attention.

LOST AND FATHERLESS

When one member gains too much influence the balance of power shifts, the system responds.

You're not like them so they hate you. There's no other reason for mistreatment from those two.

Mean, gossipy, catty using sly innuendos and a cadre of enforcers of alpha female's worldview.

SINGLE IN A SHACK

You wanna live single in a shack or have a real life of marriage and building an empire together?

Real life is not single in a shack. That's how I lived way back and I'm totally through with that.

Have pot roast ready: tricks of happy homelife thru centuries are no longer passed down see.

He works in rat race then needs tranquility. She creates happy homelife, he gets higher pay.

The fact that >HALF end in divorce explains a generation of lost kids getting off course.

A GENERATION OF LOST KIDS

Their anger over abandonment lands on those having nothing to do with it [it's hard to forget it].

Liberals always come up with exceptions to the rule and it's a speedbump making us fools.

A new generation of men seek to enslave women. Whether subtle or blatant they own you man.

They were fatherless and wimpy but thru male demagoguery joyously flipped to misogyny.

LOST AND FATHERLESS

They found relief after not having to kowtow to feminist mothers who drive ya' nuts somehow.

You keep recalling the blight of being on the bottom: use it to keep you up with bold action.

SPEAK ABOUT YOUR PLIGHT

For charisma, have brevity. Talking too much is such a turn off to the elite who can help you quickly.

Male misogyny is the natural and predictable outcome of feminism which is truly disgustin'

The natural male would be protectin' and providin' but now they're hatin'--see what you've done?

In a small town you're pegged without judge or jury. Women work it: watch out for the ladies.

There's too much mixture of the trivial with the important in your speech: delete, delete!

A rich person is not one who has the most but who needs the least: it's just psychology.

He doesn't care that you gave it to him--it's his now! He gives no credits and it's all his show.

NEW TRENDS WITH YOUNG MEN

The trend of old men with young women triggered a new trend of young men with old women.

The young men have BOSS mothers so are VERY attracted to professional female elders.

Naive. Since I didn't know what people were like I had no reason for boundaries: lucky to be alive.

LOST AND FATHERLESS

Of course God uses the internet to speak to us--why wouldn't He? But Satan's also here see.

Male misogyny is demeaning as it's based on SMV: sexual market value lost with aging.

Those without God fear aging since it's all about society not getting better until the end.

They're reacting to the devil in you not you but it sure teaches you about people, his tools.

IRRATIONAL FEAR OF AGING

Fear of aging is only about your SMV in society. Focus on homelife and this is all unnecessary.

We do our best work in our nineties then we die suddenly. No declension like others see.

If he compares you to inferior women never see him again. You come number one or none.

If you could hear her brash self promotion you'd be equally sickened. Just do your work ma'am.

Patience on acting can only make you better. Wait, prepare, don't force it or call out/prayer.

She caught him thru sex and got him to the altar, but what about his noncommitment when bored?

IT'S ABOUT LOYALTY NOT ATTRACTION

Forget attraction, Christian fidelity is about loyalty in monogamy even when she's old/homely.

Can a dam Jim Dandy narcissist be loyal like that even when he doesn't bloody FEEL it? Forget it.

LOST AND FATHERLESS

To **NOT** sin in respect to a principal [better forever with God/to **WIN**] is your strength you know.

He's not attracted to wifey so has an office affair. Feelings may change but vows make it clear.

You wanna be teacher's pet but it's best to rise above it and just do your own gifted thing direct.

Don't worry, you'll be a blank entry. Cuz of your novelty they can't see but it'll happen **SUDDENLY**.

SPEAKING TOPICS OF SYSTEM REFUGEES

Compare me to others and I'll rip you up and spit you out. I'm a Christian, an individual and odd.

If he's gonna use his bully pulpit to game you then stop listening or continue being a fool.

Childbearers [women] are tender, sensitive and empathic but the anti-female spirit is sadistic.

In WWII concentration camps the most sadistic guards by far were **WOMEN**: think about that.

Liberals are speed bumps always objecting to clear talk with "exceptions to the rule" stops.

If I'm not number one with you then you're the bottom of the totem pole with me/under my shoe.

These people are cruel, social and cannot be trusted. Tell the world about em--wait for that minute.

YOUR DESTINY IS THE HIGHEST

The thing you're meant to do will bring you the most joy when doing it so kindly stop resisting it.

LOST AND FATHERLESS

Whatever you want, fast for it. Tighten your belt, give things away, sacrifice and you'll have it.

All recovery is elimination. They talk too much and got too much stuff, that's just the beginning.

All disease is obstruction. Left to your own you'd speed on thru but now you must overcome.

All success is attraction once having eliminated obstruction and that's the whole theorem.

The system was so obtuse what the hell else could you do? Close that door and go forward Sue.

The widespread anti-whitism is an imaginary racism while true racism [anti-white] is veiled.

Constantly talking about white privilege lays the ground for violence and they know it.

COMPLETION OF CREATIVE ACT

Dependency on man is living on quicksand and sin because God wants us to depend on Him.

God didn't create you to feed you to wolves nor did He input a Creative Act to be shelved.

Relax, you've done your work now let your destiny roll out according to His plan/time to blast off.

God knows how to bless you and who to send in your life but you block it by chasing some guy.

You are blessed if you make the Lord your hope. No more living on quicksand/divine dope.

You're royalty. Royalty demands reliability and people are unreliable so that leaves God/the Able.

LOST AND FATHERLESS

She fears being nothing without him when she could be everything without him, amen.

The female community is much like a prison yard. You gotta work it constantly to survive God.

Those are her flying monkeys: alpha female would-bes who will switch sides offered more money.

It's all collusion against ONE. They collude to bring God's people down [first page of Psalms].

ELDER VISION: HOME IS GALAXY

The vision of the elder narrows down to her own home, which is actually the whole galaxy ingrown.

Along with that comes elder suspiciousness: a knowledge of psychology which is hard won miss.

So we eliminate the superfluous and evil officious and narrow down to home: eternal/delicious.

Just fast today and it takes a life of its own. Before you know it ten fasting days have gone.

START to fast: it's a spiritual thing like entering the Lord's den. See it that way and begin.

You reach a point of stalemate/nothing works. You need to amp it up and fasting comes first.

Stuck in a dream, lack of breakthrough, nothing happening. Time to fast and get real happy.

If you want special things you must fast and pray but don't tell em that, they'll cart you away.

After a period of celebratory feasting you must fast, that's just the way life works/it's a blast.

LOST AND FATHERLESS

Don't tell em your fasting, the results aren't good. It's not for approval but for success understood?

When the body itches it's time to shed it. Start to fast then brush the skin daily as it renews it.

"Coffee to wake up, booze to get drunk, water for the engine and orange juice for vitamins." Andrew Tate

Stay away from accusatory women thinking they know everything cuz they listen to The View darling.

The women seem innocent but are dangerous, getting on the horn to make you look ridiculous.

TRUST HOW THE STORY ENDS

You don't need to know how the story will end if it's Jesus on whom you depend. Relax friend.

You're not stuck in a dream, you're WAITING and preparing for that minute predestined.

I'm doing what I'm supposed to do, that's all I know. I was born to do it and so were we all.

"What do you expect to happen?" they always said. "It" I replied/what I've waited for since ten.

World Star fame which goes down in history, that's all I want for work taking half a century.

As a triple Pisces I had to experience the flip side which was devastating and weird, aye.

After paying my rightful dues for sins I came back out to the light, as pure as a little child again.

No videos to fill your life, bring out your OWN inner life by eliminating all that info/society's strife.

LOST AND FATHERLESS

You don't wanna be around youth who seem callous/uncouth. Join the club/separate for truth.

Gen clash is why elders sequester into exclusively older communities and I heartily agree.

Social trends are interesting to academicians but my focus on such is questioned by friends.

The elimination of all inessential details: that is a good speaker--cutting through as an influencer.

Stop brash self-promotion and just do your work. Much of it is deception--LYING--too you jerk.

OVERCOME FRENEMIES
How People Hold Us Down

FLYING MONKEY NETWORKS
ENVISION CARPET RIDE OUTA HERE
SO EMPTY INSIDE YOU NEED THE SNIDE?
NOT CULPRITS OR VICTIMS BUT ACTORS IN THE SYSTEM
YOU BLEW IT BUT JESUS FIXED IT
MAL-ADAPTATIONS TO TYRANNY
AVOID FICKLE FRENEMIES WHO BLOCK DESTINY
SEE WHO YOU ARE: A STAR
BULLIES USE PEER PRESSURE
PUT EM ALL IN A BAG THEN THROW IT OUT
DEDICATED TO SCAPEGOATED PATRIOTS
RESTORE OLD PATHS
ARROGANT AUDACITY MAKES MISTAKES
ELIMINATE OR EMULATE
ANYTHING FOR APPROVAL
SHIT TESTS
CONSTANT DISAPPOINTMENT
HOW YOU TREAT DISSIDENTS
CREATED FROM DESPAIR
PLEASURES OF HOME
RECOVER BY SEEING YOUR LIMITATIONS

OVERCOME FRENEMIES

How People Hold Us Down

THEY IMPOSE THEIR FRIENDS
YOUR OWN LIFE IS PURE ADVENTURE
TRUTH IS THE DOMINANT FORCE
STOP ANSWERING THE PHONE
LITTLE PEOPLE ARE MEAN
ABSURD BEHAVIOR WAS A DEMON
THE CREATIVE ACT AND AGING
ELDERING IS LUCID RECALL: LITTLE GEMS!
SWEET SOLITUDE BRINGS ORDER
PRIMED TO BE SOCIAL/HAVE MANY FRIENDS
GENIUS SUFFERS WITH CONTRADICTION
THE DARK SIDE IS CORRUPT
NO NEED TO COMPETE
FOOLISH FASHION OF FAWNING PHONIES
IT'S STRESSFUL FEELING VULNERABLE
HURRAY! YOU'VE THE ANSWER: FAST AND PRAY
CLARITY AND COMPLETION
YOU'LL HAVE A WONDERFUL LIFE
CHURCH: A BRICK TO CARRY?
SUCCESS COMES FROM GOD!
TACOS FOREVER

OVERCOME FRENEMIES
How People Hold Us Down

FLYING MONKEY NETWORKS

If a female is jealous she'll NEVER give up on her target and either you get help or leave the state: go now.

Because women fight thru flying monkeys--others in their camp, it's all about that--you face her ARMY.

I was constantly balancing factions around me associated with her and she was shrewd/a social whore.

To my Jezebel ex-friend: You are the most dangerous person I ever knew, angering your army so cruel.

Feeling powerless the female seeks sidekicks and these can be very dangerous as she directs their hits.

You are SO dangerous and unpredictable I can't even say I know you, or ever acknowledge you too.

You thought you were playing cute/clever games and I wound up destroyed and it came from your friends.

The weak narcissistic husband will assembly his flying monkey army from HER relatives, get this.

The weak sadistic husband will sense who's jealous of her and nurture that contact for a future project.

Many married people can't stand being with each other. Best to live separately but he's there to protect her.

Don't ever invite his family/kids to live with you or they'll realign against you-- the evil stepmother, cruel.

OVERCOME FRENEMIES

With blended families comes ruthless jealousies and I'd hate to know the extent of flings and cruelties.

The social wars were so intricate only moving/new marriage could open me to a new world free of all of it.

ENVISION CARPET RIDE OUTA HERE

Imagine being a billionaire and you can fly away on that magic carpet ride-- shoot for this if only in your mind.

She'd listen to her friends and run back to repeat it. Bearer of evil tidings: she's terrible trouble and not worth it.

Out of pure dumbness and lack of self-awareness she's nothing but trouble so get out now or regress.

They ask impugning questions putting you on the defensive having to explain yourself--never allow this.

Never let em hold you to your past. "Ok I was crazy but I'm not now and that's it" cuz it was paid by Christ.

Out of pure stupidity and following trends she's only trouble as she gossips about you not measuring up now.

She brags about you to them, they put you down, she changes her mind/comes back with a frown.

She's no self-awareness, only social awareness which changes constantly-- she keeps in step unquestionably.

They wanna destroy the U.S. for their lust for power, wanting to rule our lives and design utopia for all of us.

With nausea take ten raisins. They bind acid at a rate of 13 [twice the grape] and will fix the problem.

This last shit test was your Pyrrhic victory: you may have gotten an ego thrill but you lost me forever baby.

OVERCOME FRENEMIES

There's a conspiracy against privacy in social cultures. They even get violent towards introverts, the vultures!

How sad when a spiritual experience leads to a church that is so social it's frightening to the introverts.

I have a divine right to go deep inside but how is that possible with interruptions all day and night?

Introverts may eventually join a convent for privacy, only to submit to rules/regulations making em crazy.

How come only the rich and famous get privacy? Have you ever questioned that, nosy?

SO EMPTY INSIDE YOU NEED THE SNIDE?

So desperately empty on the inside you need social contact to feel alive.

Personal autonomy transcends loyalty to the group but the social animal will never understand that--shoot!

Don't call social hall religion a church! It's between God and I but you just want attention--that comes first.

It's the fact that I studied where to go and went that saves me. Do the work, you're not safe automatically.

Forget who hurt you but never what it taught you.

If you resent someone's past deeds (unforgiveness) someone else can't forgive you (it's reciprocal I guess).

I'm split: that's borderline. Or am I complex: a thinker (with many windows open to view) but always refined?

Holding on to things is so destructive. You should have progressed but are held back and unproductive.

If you have grudges (i.e. unforgiveness) you'll be haunted by your own sins with embarrassing remorse (faux pas).

OVERCOME FRENEMIES

Productive Puttering. Stay right-brained: floating from bible to dictionary to FB to looking out the window.

NOT CULPRITS OR VICTIMS BUT ACTORS IN THE SYSTEM

Stop looking at culprits as people but actors in a system--the part they played but you overcame, amen.

Since it really was the devil who made you do it, after repentance separate it in mind so you can again intuit.

The success-driven don't allow past mistakes to ruin their glow because it's Jesus they know.

Karma's comin', no bribe can block God's vindication

Justice is necessary for the relief of the saints. After being lorded over by these creeps it removes their taints.

Do not be deceived, the "most likely to succeed" can fail utterly and suddenly if repentance isn't achieved.

If you sense favoritism take joy cuz God hates unjust weights and will make it right more than mere hate.

Never speed up a dog's death cuz older dogs are the best.

Even if I didn't love you we'd still be married cuz it's about God and His covenants with the odd.

As long as you have breath, believe. Mark Helprin

They called him a stupid clown. Hah! Now he's the greatest, renowned.

Your animals will only do as well as you do--a perfect reflection of where we're at: high or blue.

Since it's all about the copy, they won't ever need to see you--unless in desperation you want to.

YOU BLEW IT BUT JESUS FIXED IT

OVERCOME FRENEMIES

He had his moment and he blew it. Not you--you blew it but then Jesus fixed it all by erasing it.

You'll fall deeper into your own reality with music, not a movie. WITH out visual it's your inner journey.

Emotional pain will always seek comfort. Drugs, shopping, porn--but it's wonder-less slumber.

All I want is protection so I can do what I do all night and day. It's about daily living: hurray.

Is he working it mentally? What does he have planned? Will he get what he wants, is it pre-ordained?

"It can be done" my father said. No matter what remember that because our Savior was bled.

We're there to protect each other's privacy. We unite in errands, projects or longer trips--it's all ok.

Don't be angry at the cad just glad you've learned all you need to know so the future is not as sad.

True wealth comes from ideas and an understanding of how things work: these bring perks.

Why is criticism/rejection the highest form of flattery? Becuz most of it comes from envy and jealousy.

Poetry is higher than writing since less is more: Potent verse is most memorizable: simple.

What I write is not about you, things just come through. I keep myself open and ready and you should too.

Lady said: they fall to the side, they hurt. Men's eyes fall there and it's not a flirt. I feel great now: elegant and perk.

Botched boob jobs are a horrific thing yet they're still churning them out in boobjob factories, ole.

OVERCOME FRENEMIES

Make yourself apt to receive: the inspiration that is, for how you live determines what you perceive.

Can't stand chemicals, cold, heat, pain/emotional drain. Total Load goes up when hurt, even the brain.

Total Load is a sliding variable based on environment so you're allergic one day but not another.

Aging is saging: Post-Adulthood is a time of enrichment, but if feared it becomes an ailment.

Americans fear aging so at thirty they start aching when they could get better yearly: blazing!

"Old" is now a good word. It means you're at the top of your game though it may seem weird.

Least words is power cuz it's memorable to the masses. Choose carefully like the brass does.

I'm compelled to rhyme in word pictures. I don't know why this compulsion but hope it pleasures.

MAL-ADAPTATIONS TO TYRANNY

Finally I just have to turn inward. Not so much outer data--I know we're in trouble but I still see far.

They criticize you and you get bigger. Resistance builds muscle as you rise up with more vigor.

Instead of wasting time hating your sister or brother focus only on world fame and helping many others.

As you keep changing creatively don't expect em to stay around, just accept the evolution of old/new systems.

We're ready to go, it's been such a long haul. We're exhausted from conflicts but now it'll be a ball

OVERCOME FRENEMIES

Plant seeds, wait to be discovered. Start the weekend on Weds. cuz your best always comes from leisure.

People are so busy socializing they can't develop their talents. It's a shame, for most it's their last chance.

Posers. A clear mind spots em instantly and that's how wisdom protects you from pain, torment and tragedy.

Great leaders are trained in pits or prisons. For me it was desert wilderness in a cabin giving joy and vision.

AVOID FICKLE FRENEMIES WHO BLOCK DESTINY

Humiliation caused by others can block your destiny. Look up, press ahead-- and avoid fickle frenemies.

An affliction, a mal-adaptation to alcoholic parents or a generational curse? I don't know but it ran it's course.

The same low life level making em messy brings other stresses. Choose upward that's what success is.

Resistance builds muscle and genius is bred in overcoming obstacles--not by slogans and making a spectacle.

You gotta be exceptionally strong to be creative cuz though tired you must always write it down or lose it.

There's only one right publisher for you, so paper your walls with rejections by fools--it's a sign you're so cool.

You've a right to total world success and justified remuneration, you've been kind to animals, that's all, amen.

For a poet it is necessary to release bursts of energy in words--by resolving contradictions, that comes first.

I have no special talents, I am just passionately curious. Albert Einstein

You've had your waterloo so now it's time to enjoy the fruits.

OVERCOME FRENEMIES

It's over, forget it. Put it all in a bag and throw it out.

Put the crazy things you did in a bag and label it "insanity" now throw the bag out cuz you resolved the tragedy.

Most rejection is ideological discrimination.

I don't give a darn what anyone thinks. I know my Waterloo and what I've been through.

Relax, you're a national treasure. Now just do your thing and don't give em any mind, they're just into pleasure.

ELIMINATE OR EMULATE

Eliminate evil--not cuz you may emulate it but because you HATE it so much your success is blocked.

When I wade thru muddy waters by listening to you chatter I get filthy mud on me because words MATTER.

You're so filled with self it isn't funny and you display it daily honey--now I'm really done with this baloney.

Getting rid of you brought clarity finally. No more ups and downs cuza your words so silly, I mean really...

You feel one with the young crowd cuza your "F" talk but for a man your age you're nothing but a fu**up.

I'm not impressed with you anymore. I've seen/heard enough to know you're not who I thought you were.

ANYTHING FOR APPROVAL

You are obviously trying to get approval of the peanut gallery and it's embarrassing honey--goodbye Mr. Silly.

Like any narcissist you're here/there/everywhere. Your moods and likes/dislikes change daily I declare.

OVERCOME FRENEMIES

I am SO glad to be rid of you and your influence. I feel so light, witty, giddy--you were the devil in me.

Such a shiny nice exterior but inside you're a haunted house to endure, I'm so glad to be free of you dear.

When love turns to hate it's very sudden for a woman--when she's de-pedestalized [finally seen] a lemon.

All I can say is Thank You Father for showing me the light on this guy. I feel so happy/free, to evil goodbye!

When a woman falls outa love it's sudden and she doesn't have to explain it to the cheating vermin.

SHIT TESTS

When they give me shit out they go because i've blocked them and now they don't EXIST no mo'

Thanks to your elimination I have a new lease on life. Everything looks so different untainted by strife.

What changed everything? A friggin' sixth sense and I don't have to explain anything if you're that dense.

When I think of you I'm disgusted--that's reason to hope for an upswing in my affairs cuz you're busted.

He's compelled to shit-test you and he lost, that's all--his cute stunt shoved back in his face cuza some doll.

Your ego shit-tested me and it came right back to thee. You make me sick now--the correct response, see?

Shit-test a smart woman and DEEP feelings switch suddenly and you never get em back again buddy.

It would be demeaning to me to even go to your page now. At deepest levels I know this, confirmed by God.

OVERCOME FRENEMIES

Compelled to shit-test, suffers major loss. That's how Satan does us in: he urges meanness, you lose the best.

Narcissist is compelled to shit test you. If you accept it he gets worse, if you don't he's shocked/get nervous.

Tell em to shut up--the reason you're so good is cuza your age. They treat it like a disease, tho' a sage.

Don't worry baby, the bigger they [think they] get the harder they will fall cuz NO one's that good after all.

His friggin' shiny exterior over an empty vessel/mean interior will come out as it always has historically dear.

It's YOU that has it not that empty vessel/shiny fake mongrel. Remember that, get back into that and float UP!

Don't let that creep get ahead! GOD SAID: He'd bring ONE up as He brings the OTHER down: that's success.

CONSTANT DISAPPOINTMENT

The constant disappointments tromping thru the mud! That's what it was like bud and what a dud.

If you go back to him you're not a smart/independent woman you're an emo-traumatized victim.

Why would I ENVY? It's not a finite pie. We all have a part to play and I admire genius when I see it eye to eye.

She wanted marriage, you didn't so she went elsewhere, why resent it? You went solo so why be so low?

You glorified zen singleness but she wanted more from life so married another guy but why do you cry?

Marriage IS attachment so if you're into new age/Hindu crap why wouldn't she drop your ass and reattach?

OVERCOME FRENEMIES

Everything you say is a lie perverting/misdirecting the guys and every day it's more obvious: goodbye.

Women are savage beasts because they've born to compete and from this they become sadists with ease.

A secret of happiness is to UP the level of not caring. These things are ephemeral/soon there's no memory.

First I earned the right to stay home all the time THEN I became a meticulous housekeeper sublime.

First I got rid of everything THEN I was called the "meticulous housekeeper like the palace of a Queen".

I don't give a dam about anything out there cuz in HERE is where it's all at for me, a queen on her chair.

HOW YOU TREAT DISSIDENTS

The way you treat dissidents marks you as a cult. We don't like it and if you persist you'll surely fall.

A female writer comes to success in her home. That's the historical imperative and it makes sense no?

Love is shown in five ways: quality time, words of affirmation, physical touch, gifts and acts of service.

A smart women isn't just reacting a WORDS but the WORLDS of meaning behind em/suddenly the thrill is gone.

You were just my Ph.D. in the Streets. Other than that you have no meaning, a mere legion entity.

It's all synchronicity baby--can you hold on a little longer maybe?

The older female's not dominant, she's a rudder for his ship--and that's why her husband makes it big.

OVERCOME FRENEMIES

Too hot, too fast and sudden fall. Take it gradually step by step and things will last a lot longer for y'all.

Am I making a judgement about his filthy nonproductive past times? Yes, I guess I am doing just that.

No wonder you're disgusted with adults--they're all neurotic. They bought the trip and you're the culprit.

No wonder I was disgusted with adults--they all went along with that crap, always opposing my map.

Let the past break down like a comical dream. Altho' tragic, recall it's a system/things aren't what they seem.

CREATED FROM DESPAIR

The reason I'm this way today is because I've seen the other side of reality and it frightened me eternally.

There's nothing more frightening than medical tyranny cuz they can come and get you and you're history.

I hate to tell you this but the sweet stench in democrat leftist districts is the crap of dust mites in bum piss.

It's all settled now, let things fall into place but just remember who's the ace in this relationship: Jesus.

They were total imbeciles--just social. As though there was no division between each other: mobs are awful.

In The Golden Girls the slut was made to look cute. Many women emulated Blanche then lost their loot.

With medical tyranny millions were killed in Nazi Germany. With one sweeping law, you're dead/history.

My parents are eternally grateful I brought them to Christ. That's what the bible says tho' they've passed.

OVERCOME FRENEMIES

The basement is the most important room. Put everything in it then penuriously select what goes in your home.

When destiny and the changing of the guard and seasons is written on the wall like this, why resist it?

Spent a week ordering every drawer. I've eliminated all superfluity or unnecessary, an orderly home is power.

I don't know if its cowardice or just waiting on God. I believe in God's TIMING to the exact minute/second.

Even when you say NO people will pressure you to leave home saying "it'll do you good" but it's all bull.

NOTHING out there comes close to what's in here and it doesn't interest me one bit so shut up dear.

PLEASURES OF HOME

Nothing compares to the pleasures of home so when they pressure you to leave refuse their syndrome.

They act like it's a disease staying home NEVER to roam. They even call it the "Social Anxiety Syndrome".

You were my Ph.D. in the Streets imposing on me with all your creeps and thoughts and attitudes which stink.

When you really don't give a shit you won't have a need to constantly say you don't give a shit.

STOP pressuring me. When I say NO I mean no. Now I sound like an angry mother but it's just logic you know.

You raised your voice/rose up like you were going to hit me: that's how I was controlled before awakening.

I hate social occasions with a passion. They size me up, they look me up and down, I read the minds of Oz.

OVERCOME FRENEMIES

No I'm not gonna answer a silly question in your matrix. I'm just gonna state the truth then escape this.

All the forty-something generation can say is "IT'S AMAZING" and it's really getting sickening.

I hate social occasions with a passion. They size me up, they look me up and down, I feel imposed upon.

RECOVER BY SEEING YOUR LIMITATIONS

To recover from ALL addictions I had to realize my limitations. Without the social I healed right up, free again.

Some people are so complex they can't handle intricate social signals and what they see makes em freak out.

A truly woke lady knows the basis of that remark, the hidden attack of a shark and how it harms.

They don't want me to happily stay home--they want me on THEIR turf unprotected by my leisurely comforts.

Someone who reads all their minds, are you kidding? They won't walk into a crowd of any kind intentionally.

So now you know how to order and stock your home and who to stay away from so you can become renowned.

Too much partying, drinking and drugging will ruin your destiny. Take it from me, repent to be free.

Stop worrying about that person, draw a boundary and you're done. Stop reliving history that was no fun.

Stop thinking about her--draw a line. She gets others against you: your lesson about social swine.

After each project FOCUS you must return to center. A couple days of music/movies and you're there.

OVERCOME FRENEMIES

THEY IMPOSE THEIR FRIENDS

My relationship is with you not all your dam friends. But due to your big mouth I'm done anyway--the end.

All I can recall about you is the HORROR of you constantly imposing your friends on me: go away freak.

Your friends were all mad at me, they hated me! It dawned on me why this was: your endless gossiping.

Gossip networks around females are so intricate one must geographically relocate to nip it in the bud.

SEE WHO YOU ARE: A STAR

Not only do they constantly ask favors, then you have to go to a "thank you" dinner you don't want either.

The truth has a certain ring to it. When people hear it they know it's true so don't fear em and keep speaking it!

All crazy behaviors were a mal-adaptation to them (liberal thought) so just forget it all as a lie you bought.

The purer we get the grosser our sins look. Everyone has that, forget it you kook.

Say it boldly with certitude and you're confronted with "not always". That's how they make us weak nowadays.

My alpha was put to sleep and the pack reassembled. It's Systems Theory: same with humans despite the devil.

Dogs know.

BULLIES USE PEER PRESSURE

Bullies use peer pressure. We have the thinkers they have the stinkers.

OVERCOME FRENEMIES

Trump wins again simply by the left losing it's mind: it's ethics, dignity/self-control--it was awesome! Greg Gutfeld

Trump drew them right into his trap--he's so fab!

Due to their breakneck insatiable addiction to ratings they went ahead (integrity be damned) with out checking.

Relax, your persecutors are now old prunes. Things change and you gotta evolve--that's forgiveness too.

Can't get over the years unprotected. Marriage changed all that and it's like a wall to flourish with the elected.

She's embarrassingly self-involved and boring, but these garish narcissistic displays draw men in, adoring.

That's the social hypnotic: bringing shame for being unique. It's not true, they're the conformist freaks.

Sheila was influenced by her female friends to get a divorce. It only takes a few to ruin life/bring a curse.

God's discipline can be brutal but after repentance a joyous renewal.

Sometimes the less you work the more you accomplish—that's the creative, joyous.

Productive puttering produces the most.

The true sign of intelligence is not knowledge but imagination. Albert Einstein

Nothing feels so good as a buzzcut, that's why I wear it bud.

There's nothing worse than a woman's scorn. Poor men, as women vent ugly anger and husbands are forlorned.

I make her beautiful and she loves me in return. Plastic Surgeon

Rich: but if you think you'll get a dime you're outa your mind cuz I recall before you were no friend of mine.

OVERCOME FRENEMIES

To find yourself think for yourself and only trust those with proven track records (friends who never sold out).

How happy it makes me that life can be reduced to simple things like rain.

The only people you can trust are those who don't need anything from you and they're hard to find, that's true.

Everyone needs something so if you have ambitious people around you're in real trouble as a leader, yes sir.

Success is a stale finale, the struggle is the success. Eugene O'Neill

Resistance builds muscle/overcoming makes us stunning and it's slimming.

You're not great. No one knows you cuz you're not worthy of knowing.

You're not born great/worthy of knowing. You gotta build it and purify (glowing).

PUT EM ALL IN A BAG THEN THROW IT OUT

Put em all in the same bag: all the ridiculous actions from wrong thinking and never think of any one again.

I know movies are good but music will take you higher. It's about you (not tracking) so turn it on/aspire.

"I saw them as cruel, indifferent, callous people and it made me hurt in my stomach"--launching ED/being sick.

Micro-attention: go inside to exploding universes, freed from outer chaos of tracking details which are useless.

How can the mother homeschool the child if she has to work cuz she left her husband, advised by a jerk?

Even though they're so stupid (a blank slate) and don't react to what you say you must continue on today.

It does not matter how slowly you go as long as you do not stop. Confucius

OVERCOME FRENEMIES

You've gotta love something, it's a higher call. So love Jesus and your pets, forgetting posers one and all.

Jesus listened to me then I read the bible and it was He talking just to me re: a mess from which He set me free.

You're set free once you give up on anyone else and just go to Jesus then He opens the spout—wowee!

Only person who answered my call was Jesus who's also God. He rescued me from a mess/human mob.

I go through things just to write about it I guess.

Life became too too much and I wanted to die. That's when I turned to Jesus and He brightened my life.

After chaos my only thought was Jesus and it enveloped me as I flew off from that heartbreak over and out.

Now that you're whole, don't go back into the human drama. Instead look ahead to the future and heaven.

DEDICATED TO SCAPEGOATED PATRIOTS

To the scapegoated patriots across the land, divided from their clan due to ideology (facts be damned).

Once you come to Jesus people lose importance. Moths in the night, a wide path to hell, very little substance.

Betrayal from someone you trusted hurts the worst, that's why the Psalms is so relieving, putting that at first.

You're people-obsessed and they aren't worth it! People-worship is a sin so worship He who was sent/you'll love it.

Our strength, wisdom and power comes from the Lord and savior Jesus Christ.

Your True Self is eclipsed by the diverse multitude some crude/lewd/rude.

OVERCOME FRENEMIES

I work from 3 to 10 a.m. Then it's out to the sun and gardening/walking with my three dogs, amen.

Even if I didn't love him, he's my husband and that's the point--it's a loyalty to God so He can anoint.

Your true family may not make logical sense (it's just the one you're assigned to) and friends are few.

Due to chemical injury you're allergic to everything and called a hypochondriac but just get the facts.

It's about projection of an introjection and it's how family sickness infects future generations.

Don't deify children or they'll live up to it by creating a false self making sick evil elves.

When self-loathing sets in--for whatever reason--we create a false self and to our destiny it's treason.

Poets are higher than writers cuz least words is like an atom bomb on the dumb.

Genius knows: You gotta take a break. That means to cut it off for the day, for your family's sake.

The key to creativity is to allow your life to meander. Like an unplanned day of play, it's the facilitator.

As a poet I gotta be alone. Away from others in my own separate reality--this is my throne.

If you're not prepared don't say you rely on God. He said the wise escape but the wicked get the rod.

Money doesn't bring wisdom. In fact it facilitates big problems cuz there's no holes barred to doom.

RESTORE OLD PATHS

OVERCOME FRENEMIES

It Can Be Done. Post-sixty is the top of your game. Keep goin', you've never been better/deserve fame.

You are just a conduit to the Creative Act now. Be supple in God's hands: Forget ego, forget friends.

God is so good, He's giving me a party! We're having a blast with the Almighty.

They've got cancer cures and instead they're running eugenics programs like putting fluoride in the water?

If people respect you they respect you have your own life but that won't happen if you cave to their device.

They rob you of your most important asset: time. Because left alone you could make it big (it's a crime).

You've a destiny and every moment is important. Don't waste it, you're unequally yoked and bugged/constant.

Get a housekeeper if you can't do it on your own. That's no disgrace it's a big house for heaven sakes.

Every moment is a divine design. Don't miss the magical moment or remain as-yet-unrecognized/unrefined.

Your enthusiasm is energy--the power of focusing on what excites you--all blocked by people around you.

Stop thinking people are nice. That's your biggest mistake causing so much trouble at way too high a price.

We're all sinners so what do you expect when mankind loses all decency and lines: evil grossness/unrefined.

We all have episodes and it's unfortunate when caught on camera folks.

ARROGANT AUDACITY MAKES MISTAKES

OVERCOME FRENEMIES

Arrogant and audacious: As always, since they're out of grace they overplay their hand and make mistakes.

Virtue signaling but never forgiving, setting rules, dominant/unrelenting.

When in sin God blocks the creative spout. Dead, empty, vacuous, pat, silly, repetitive, rest on laurels--you're out.

Eldering: Mining the past for pearls should be fascinating not embarrassing. It's not aging it's saging.

Mine the past for wisdom, that's the glory of your elder days. It's fascinating to endlessly muse and it pays.

Kids are pegged with mental illnesses which they wear like a badge of honor instead of becoming geniuses.

I started eldering at 35. I let the social go, transcended it all, entered a world of thought and grew tall.

Political Science isn't just about government but family, marriage, neighborhood, klatch or club.

My mal-adaptation to liberalism started at twelve and only now am I free but I remember it all too well.

It was war: like all wars you don't suffer every memory but put it all in the same bag--to throw away and far.

When relief finally comes it's hard to believe (got used to trouble) but God said he'd reward us double.

Like war, don't go back to any part of it--put it all in a bag (stops memories from plaguing you like a nag).

The orgasmic "like" is a sign we've degraded significantly from previous generations of just being high.

Repentant: In the groove, smooth. Sin: missing, grating, something to prove.

OVERCOME FRENEMIES

Never give in to intimidations to be social. Compared to your own life it's pure commotion, boring, low level.

Pets love music (mathematics) not TV (cacophonous) so have a heart and adjust your life accordingly, thanks.

YOUR OWN LIFE IS PURE ADVENTURE

Your own life is pure adventure. Nothing compares: you're missing out by not staying home/going to affairs.

Between us and them is a huge chasm. There is no compromise and this division (in reality) has only begun.

Don't feel guilty for total privacy. It's a mark of superiority though they can never admit that, addicted to society.

You don't make a million first then become a writer. You invest decades of unpaid work while being slighted.

Forget agents and just do your work, clean your act and wait for the universe to court your (and it's sure).

Letting go expands and liberates your life. It's not less it's more as it makes you alert, energetic, creative and high.

Risen up by God to do a job.

With eldering the temporal lobes burst open to reveal eternity: wow this is bliss, power and sagacity.

The best leadership training is having to adapt to idiots: learning to stay steady in stress with out having fits.

I hate all social occasions (a terrible drag). All I wanna do is stay home and be alone and I'm never going back.

Since life is eternal, photos are soul-snatchers.

That's what I have a husband for, to smooth things over.

OVERCOME FRENEMIES

With photo-recognition software they can find you anywhere.

I just wanna stay home with my cats and dogs.

They've found sex and music hit the same brain centers. Music's the background of my life: transference?

Before you learned it you didn't know it. So quit beating yourself up because you blew it, now you're a shoe in.

TRUTH IS THE DOMINANT FORCE

We are the dominant force (the truth), not them. But go anywhere and there on TV is fake news CNN.

A left-brained female angry with a right-brained male for not remembering Valentines or other days.

The right-brained don't live in time or dates. Eternity is timeless and that's why heaven is bliss--can't wait.

Einstein's major interest was "what is eternity?" and found it's where "there is no time nor space" (field theory).

Social expectations are brutal and many break up over em, feeling it's their right with you under their thumb.

They aren't individually coming up with this crap. It's an echo chamber as they parrot the party line/map.

Man has concupiscence: a tendency towards lust--he loves his sins.

Love and help people but when they ask ridiculous favors draw that line: you have your own life friends of mine.

Without boundary-assertion people will mow you over. Draw that line, live your own life but be kind/a lover.

If people ask ridiculous favors they don't respect that you have your own life and you are not their savior.

OVERCOME FRENEMIES

All I wanna do is what I wanna do not what you want me to do so please get a life while your pleas I'll echew.

Genius remains as-yet-unrecognized owing to all the interruptions from people even those despised.

It's not "Christian" to be someone's fool/slave cuz they'll use you to your grave. Practice saying no/be brave.

"No" is the most important word in our language cuz it opens up your world. "Yes" closes it down: horror.

Life of a yes-man is a miserable watered down wasteland while those who say "NO!" have fascination/fun.

"No!" is a rocket-launcher into personal success. "Yes" is unnecessary entanglement and a mess.

Yes-people must practice saying "NO!" for it brings guilt at first. Then they get into it and feel joy/not cursed.

The hardest thing to do in a social society is establish your own boundaries--to be happy and finally free.

STOP ANSWERING THE PHONE

Stop answering the phone--ever--and just call back who you want. Stop being a victim they just wanna talk.

You've learned to manage your network now so sit and muse, write it down, never come back to the blues.

Man prefers to believe what he prefers to be true. Francis Bacon

People upward. If you don't they drag you down hell-ward.

Don't substitute destiny for little people, some evil. Seek fame which is ecstasy cuz you're an eagle.

The problematic memory is associated. with fear/threat. Realize that and memory is extinguished just like that.

OVERCOME FRENEMIES

Don't blame the little people--it was you who got entangled on that level and became mentally feeble.

There IS a hierarchy and if you think there isn't you'll act like them: limp, odd, mean, dependent, wayward, dumb.

Thinking we're all the same makes men level off to mediocrity and F-bombs to be popular though it's lame.

Since it's fear and threat that maintains the noxious memory, relax, learn to love and it goes away naturally.

Little people are social and terrified to be alone. All symbols no substance, they wanna topple your throne.

There's a hierarchy: the strong seek solitude, the inferior seek company and that's the human race to me.

LITTLE PEOPLE ARE MEAN

The little people are mean: careless, despicable, ingrown--but you are big in spirit and that's your throne.

Little people can't hurt you as long as you never forget who's who.

Don't dare criticize the little (despicable) people to your professor he'll bash you as the bigoted aggressor.

Cease feeling embarrassment and remorse for past repented sins: Think of them as mal-adaptive contaminations.

Your dog's life totally changed cuza you. YOU in-fill your dog with reality so his life is rich, full/happy not blue.

The saddest thing is when you give a pet away--to what? Do you even know? Back to the shelter is not-ok.

Is your life all about adapting to interruptions? Or do you have a locked gate with you determining your fate?

Allow people to be gone (don't go back), they're in the wrong.

OVERCOME FRENEMIES

You get to success through tedious daily actions. Never forgetting, always perfecting until moment of getting.

When in sin every demon in hell comes against you--through those you knew--but Jesus saves: whew!

RX for life: Geographically relocate, change diet.

They must be satisfied with my presence not constant affections cuz this necessary work gets all my attention.

I can't help it if they're too dumb to understand.

Arrogant people think they're invincible with you under their sway--ok?

You know you're superior so just stop trying. You're already there so just be a child joyously playing.

ABSURD BEHAVIOR WAS A DEMON

When your behavior was so absurd you can't believe it it had to be a demon and this is relieving.

Don't focus on your detractors, think only of God. Think of your perfect victory not the flawed.

Karma for narcissists: Being dumped after buttered up after that's what you did all your life, huh!

It just so happens: that just as you begin the last phase of completion utter chaos enters too, hon.

Your conscience is so seared you lose your sense of sin then that becomes a magnet to the trash bin.

Success comes from taking an obscure point and bringing it central--a simple change of view.

Take a break! Allow your own world to illuminate. Relax and enjoy three days free of all flakes.

OVERCOME FRENEMIES

Take three days off and just do music. Look out the window: dream, muse.

When things break down you gotta be strong enough not to take it on. Be yourself, hon'.

Love me, I'm always on your heart. Hate me, I'm always on your mind: I win both times.

I adhere to principals not feelings. Principals like fidelity and loyalty are truly healing.

It's amazing how prolific I get when the T.V.'s down: Turn it off/keep it off or stay dumb.

THE CREATIVE ACT AND AGING

Your remorse over eras when you were controlled by the devil: It's erased along with all evil.

So you're a fossil, so what? We're told to restore the old paths so get rid of the smut.

They come through my mind then I make em rhyme--it's a compulsion of mine.

The Creative Act: It's like building the Taj Mahal--entails great attention to detail.

Old age should not be decline but amplification: become your best, reach your apex, go to heaven oh yes!

The Creative Act is a baby you carry for decades then you finally give birth and it's recognized by the world.

I was born to do it. God put it in me before my birth and I was driven to do just that though very persecuted.

Becoming aware of mortality--not feeling invincible anymore--is the road to genius/sainthood/loving God more.

No need to apologize to the little people for dis-attention/not relating, they'll know by this your greatness.

OVERCOME FRENEMIES

I want thought triggered by music and beautiful home with it's spectacular surroundings. Dogs, neighbors and things.

Our lives changed forever cuz we went to the shelter to pick up a little monster whom we'll love forever.

Aging is when the temporal lobes burst open to reveal eternity which is panoramic vision for you and me.

ELDERING IS LUCID RECALL: LITTLE GEMS!

The elder spends his time in lucid recall of the past which he mines for "gems"--it's so much fun, friends.

I started eldering at 35. From civilization I took the dive and went to the desert wilderness as my spirit revived.

The less the superior man does the more he gets done.

Veil lifted from my eyes and new life started that minute, free of the confusion of being taken out of my limits.

We need a daily escape. Music, sit in sun, read a novel.

Since movies track the mind, I'd avoid em. Music opens: the less tracking the more we love em.

To get to success you may have to outlive people causing the mess.

What does a saint do? On high things he meditates--looks lazy to type A's.

Look out the window, this is working: let the mind go.

Mom said "looking out the window isn't working" until I got straight A's in absolutely everything.

Before gaining wisdom all of life is projection.

Vindication is necessary for the relief of the saints.

OVERCOME FRENEMIES

It's a phase of life where the bottom becomes top and the top the bottom when life goes rotten.

I use the prophets to cut them down with my words. My judgment strikes like lightning. Hosea 6:5

Fill your paper with the breathings of your heart. William Wordsworth

It's not movies but music. The less tracking your mind while it reels off to space, it's fantastic!

SWEET SOLITUDE BRINGS ORDER

In sweet solitude I was invaded by a gang of boys ruined by PC culture in the schools--they were so cruel.

It's liberal culture in California that stank. It's infested throughout so I moved to Utah and God I will always thank.

You're lazy so won't study deeply to give yourself other factors other than complaining/it's annoying.

This is just Labeling Theory: you've become their stupid label or paradigm, a lazy human tragedy.

Answer to teen depressants: man up and accept the truth.

You earn happiness through hard work and good choices. It depends on how life is lived, regardless.

They reel off diseases making them special, something we never understood when things were normal.

Don't talk about your private life, tastes, affections. Leave that out, be a mystery, be God's perfection.

Walk the common miles (the herd) or be a milestone (hard work). Socially waste time or get perks.

I don't care about you, no one cares about you. Get over yourselves, no one's stopping you.

OVERCOME FRENEMIES

The superior man avoids hostile environments, stays home and remains inaccessible--that's his value.

Many who were hit only once by dad relate to those beaten daily. This is wrong and ruins lives, surely.

I can forgive anything once but a habit? That's a dunce.

PRIMED TO BE SOCIAL/HAVE MANY FRIENDS

They primed us to be social/have many friends. Yet we're never more lonely cuz God comes first/can't pretend.

Maslow shows the most mentally healthy people have <5 friends in life. God, solitude/creativity is how they survived.

They don't take our restraint as strength but weakness--so now we'll show em who they really are, a sickness.

Victims of childhood sex abuse act out promiscuously and abuse substances: this explains a lot, ok?

People whose identity was violated as children create a false glittering seductive personna = downfall.

Don't feel sorry, it's a wide path to hell.

Don't give up, roll over and die. Look at the stars at night, kiss your mate, plant a garden, unplug from lies.

Friends are rare and they're probably not here.

It's not that someone's "bad" but man has two sides and he's stuck down in a rut (the cad can't expand).

You've a right to be cocky after all that.

Any false self/fake personna brings itself down. Only by being in groove with God (peculiar) will you be renowned.

All men are sinners and no one is perfect.

OVERCOME FRENEMIES

A weak female implodes in the Wife of the Alcoholic Syndrome. Constant insults creates hellholes not home.

Way to work: Sit, look out window, let mind do the traveling, act.

Lord lift this burden regarding book. I wanna dance, sing, forget the whole thing especially what it took.

I found my groove, it's what I do. I don't know why, can't explain it, but it just feels right and true.

GENIUS SUFFERS WITH CONTRADICTION

I always suffered with contradiction. Tho' most can tolerate it, I was driven to explain then transcend it.

If music triggers thrills with deep emotion it means you're smarter but in most it does nothing.

A monastic, austere, simple and humble life eventually pays off. Separate means holy = blast off!

Recognize simplicity is mature. Most are lost in a sea of boring words cuz they're not self-assured.

You don't fail cuza the system. You're in the freest country in the world, get off your lazy bums.

The fact no one cares should propel you to build your own life and ignore the rest: get going/have flair.

You are not a victim. Take control of your own life and become an adult, do you think you can?

Oh, the things we did under social hypnotism, but what is possible released from mind control.

Life is but a speck on a long line stretching through eternity. It's just a test: will you choose He?

OVERCOME FRENEMIES

When people become evil continually God takes em out--everything even their cities and crops.

Social? Our own life is important too and it means solitude.

Some of you need to edit your work more. It's your personal style we're talking about, so I implore.

THE DARK SIDE IS CORRUPT

Tuning to the dark side may give limited power up front but will destroy you in the process: corrupt.

If caught in discordance food/booze/drugs takes greater importance cuz it's a deep hole inside us.

You become what you follow, if disgusting you get shallow.

I've been thinking about that, all those things. Cuz PTSD's only felt after, in safety from underlings.

They didn't care about a thing, it was awful. They intruded desiring and I learned about the unlawful.

What they do is pat, mediocre and contrived. It doesn't come through them like when God is behind it.

All elders feel remorse for past sins from the 70-80s when all lines went down in a human tragedy.

Were you insane or possessed? Either way you should let it go, because you just weren't at your best.

With all lines trashed we got smashed.

Repentance brings continuous cleverness and it's revelatory so God gets all the glory of course.

Best reason to be the boss I've found: so people in unworthy positions can't boss you around.

OVERCOME FRENEMIES

God always gives a chance for reprieve (Like Jonah at Ninevah) so repent please.

God didn't bless me being alone. I had to achieve marriage and stay whole.

Relieve yourself of the whole burden of TV news. Stop, start, chat, smile: not quite true and makes ya coo coo.

Never ask, let them see God's glory in you then they'll provide (produce) the light in which you bask.

NO NEED TO COMPETE

No need to compete, we're all in our own stream I think.

If I stay with em they'll simmer down but they gotta let me work and that's creative life with dogs all around.

No need to fight with husband to see things your way. Just be an exemplar and he'll switch/all will be ok.

Best dogs began as irascible troublemaking brats. This energy channeled through discipline created the best.

Dogs sense inner rumblings when we can't. If pets are acting different an earthquake may be imminent.

Divine spirit: don't break it, channel it. Kill it and it falls from grace--disgraced--so nurture it/watch it.

Marriage is the greatest freedom for a woman.

Wisdom is learning to go with your gut.

It's a free will universe. You hold on to an idea that's true and it will win hands down every time, of course.

Things are happening so fast of course you can't review it all so just move through creatively or delete it all.

Mysticism, infantilization, psychosis, senility and creativity look alike.

OVERCOME FRENEMIES

I'm powerful in my own home with gate locked.

What they call insanity is actually a spiritual emergency as stuff comes up from collective unconscious and history.

You must beat this then get bigger.

Why waste time on youtube when 90% of it is so boring. You're above all this Karen Kellock Ph.D. my darling.

They've portrayed marriage to be a terrible, boring, useless thing and so for five decades painful divorces were rising.

Don't go to trouble for looks--silly fashions that are totally dysfunctional. Avoid trends: just your style, original.

So serious in her performances but so jocular in her interviews, it's jarring-- what gives? It's weird too.

FOOLISH FASHION OF FAWNING PHONIES

The herdling makes a fool of himself following fashion. It's not class or elegance but selfhood gets a glance.

At this stage I'm not interested in a flashy man, rich man, educated man but a loyal consistent stable man.

Not rich or educated but loyal and compassionate that's the best

People are deliberately cruel, thinking it's cool.

We have this place, today. We're together in this destiny. Donald Trump

There's something called facial recognition software where they can find you anywhere. That's why I don't post pics dear.

The path of genius is productive puttering. All day long without a plan but write it down after musing/muttering.

Just wake me up when it's all over. Skip the endless details or other setups to distract from my divine makeover.

OVERCOME FRENEMIES

Silence maintains your own happy reality. Silence conforms to every surface it meets in perfect synchrony.

Marriage gave me freedom to be cuz I was protected, see? Women need men cuz there's no true equality.

Mental Health Prescription in latter days of chaos: Bonanza, Big Valley, Turner Classic Movies, take the day off.

My role: For those who care to know I've laid it all out in whole.

All day it's Turner Classic Movies. This mental transport makes me so happy--time capsules opening to eternity.

You seem like you hate me telling you what to do but you told me to.

IT'S STRESSFUL FEELING VULNERABLE

It is stressful feeling vulnerable. To get the world give it up. Synchronicity = you/your work fits in history.

I was jealous of him/her until I saw there is no competition for the winners are the repentant.

It wasn't great, it made her irate but it was the Queen's Disease/her fate.

Please realize how important you are to your dog/cat: stay put.

Forward: at the front, ahead, advanced, onward, prompt, ready, bold, presumptuous, futuristic.

I want things neat all the time or as a cerebrotonic I feel disorderly and crazy.

The good thing about money is you can do your own thing/not be beholden to anybody.

The magic carpet ride is: being rid of the past. This psychic opening is a blast.

The past has abnormal control over the present so just learn what you must and good riddance.

OVERCOME FRENEMIES

"It just is": So long as divorce is an option you're always doubting and looking around.

Nothing works but Jesus. That's why you're unhappy and keep tryin' to please us.

I wanna look at the view. I wanna see weather and take in all of God's nature too.

Obstructions of people, habit and food muck up the works—make us indifferent or jerks.

My insecurities compel constant improvement and that's why I work every single moment.

I can't take any more, just listen to music. It's horrible what's happening but God said praise it.

Let no one tell you how to do it. Get the gist then on it put your twist and that's the perfect fix.

Poet: political-psychological pundit I guess you'd call it and that's cuz I know it having gone through it.

I don't care what anyone says. This is true maturity: it's the True Self and God who created it, always.

I'll get the main headlines but all these details I'll let go cuz life is a pie and it's my groove I'll refine.

I've come to just appreciate what I see out my window. In situ: just my own situation, ya know.

I don't care about the movie I just want it to evoke thought in me. I stop it often to write and think.

She doesn't inspire me to wear a bikini, just to be the best I can be and that also means physically.

HURRAY! YOU'VE THE ANSWER: FAST AND PRAY

OVERCOME FRENEMIES

Hurray! You have the answer: Fast and pray. It's so easy/costs nothing as it saves the day.

So what if he's a cute kid--Satan uses the shy and sheepish. Don't judge by appearances, Paul admonishes.

If they don't come when they say nor put things back in place they're immature/still a baby face.

My bruised adult ego still won't let go but I'll pray about it and see if they are someone I should know.

Get past looks. For some that's all it took as they settle down to solid and stable life (no deception/strife).

Never trust people who stand you up. Even once is a no-brainer: a sign of disrespect/dumb schmucks.

Now is the time for System Inversion (enantiodromia) as the bottom becomes the top--oh my!

You had yours, now it's my time to shine. We'll all disappear but for now, seasons of cheer (no beer).

She always just escaped me, she was never there. Ended in a rest home and then she disappeared.

I honestly can't take it anymore. I've done my part now I just wanna explore my own inner journey with art galore.

Just remember the most important comes first. That's what gets attention and makes them read further.

The Creative Act is a baby you carry for decades then you finally give birth and it's recognized by the world.

Celebrate your success before it happens. Create the mood, man: happiness!

Mom said just wear what I have on. Synchronicity not put-ons (be gone).

OVERCOME FRENEMIES

One never knows when he'll be done until that moment he's done. Albert Einstein

CLARITY AND COMPLETION

This is the last brick in the building: completion of the creative act. If you're willing, it's a whole new life in fact.

Few have opportunity to pursue their talents. Problems in their network or false ideas and they lose all chance.

Home: Obama and cronies aren't here and out there Donald will take care of it, our dear. Relax, not a tear.

All that matters is you love it. Doesn't matter what they think, if they like it or even if they hate all of it.

To an inner genius or the saints the outer world is loud, noisy, cacophonous, irritating and disorderly.

Don't get messed up with emotional entanglements and jealousy triangles from situations long ago.

You can be eclipsed by another human as an overshadowing influence: Spirit crushed, mind a dunce.

The sexes need each other. For example females have a problem with completion/need male vision.

A good marriage is 2 + 2 = 20,000. It's dynamite, the royal couple and it means wealth and elation.

You reach your peak and then you decline--so what? We all have a place in the sun at a certain date and time.

So much wasted time worrying when soon you will be dead. Why not make a mark instead--get out the lead.

Nothing fascinates like your own mind. You've forgotten that filling time.

Intelligence, audacity, cleverness.

OVERCOME FRENEMIES

Make yourself "apt" to receive. Sit down, look out the window, believe.

Wow, I can leave the chaos and just float on Holy Spirit Ease, productive puttering with dear Lord Jesus.

YOU'LL HAVE A WONDERFUL LIFE

Personally it's turning out to be a wonderful time. Everything's coming together beautifully as if divine.

First they ignore, then they laugh, then they fight you and then you win. Gandhi "The obstacle is the path."

Just cuz you have nothing to hide doesn't mean they can't set you up. We have reason to fear but look up.

Substitute love for dead logs who couldn't care less for the eternal Jesus and forget the dying moths, the godless.

Love takes sacrifice but they're all about "getting my needs met". Sickening, truly. I worry about kids/pets.

Crippled in the free market because they don't know how to fail, reason, write, think or debate.

Helpless victims become vicious abusers. Greater the childhood trauma the greater the addiction.

We've had a dose of female logic in Pelosi, Watters, Clinton and the future is ruled by same warped vision.

Let no one tell you how to do it. You were born for it but needed to grow into it and that took ruin.

To be a success all you need is finish high school, be married before babies, get a job. Ben Shapiro

Marriage is a divine institution. Being alone's not good but joining forces makes life a celebration.

OVERCOME FRENEMIES

If you're smart but with the wrong premise or principals you can reason your way to your own funeral.

CHURCH: A BRICK TO CARRY?

I always loved the Lord but couldn't stand when church became a brick to carry not a lamp to guide/bored.

Sin is a device to deal with anxiety. It works for awhile then the serpent turns back to strike with insanity.

Don't tell me to go anywhere, it's flawed. It's boring, tedious or debauched and I just wanna be with God.

Disorder reflects mind. Clear minds can't stand it--they want clarity, beauty, order from chaos: the refined.

You're outa sorts from someone in your network. Cut em loose, that's the power of disengagement, it works.

Heck, disinherit the jerks.

You must be mentally free to think, talk and write so get em out of your perception: no more silly P.C.!

Since I was a grasshopper in their eyes I became a grasshopper. I got strong and unswayable when I got older.

The saints show an unheard of level of courage in public. William James

Everyone knows clean order is superior to dirty disorder, or do they?

Music is everything to me. It makes me think, how to be more free.

Genius mistrusts words.

Poets work alone in the home. Words are what I do and it's best when they are few.

Poets work 24/7/365 cuz it's their whole life sorting out strife.

OVERCOME FRENEMIES

It's not up to the publisher or useless agent--it's up to God!

SUCCESS COMES FROM GOD!

Success doesn't come from the east or west but from God who puts one down and the other up: the best.

It's what you do and it doesn't matter if they understand it or if there is no money from it.

Make your mundane world absurd. Unveil the magic--see between the lines and behind all their many words.

You get to a point where you can taste success. When that golden ring comes around (again) don't miss!

Christian women learn how not to hate the husband but love him, amen? Our tendency is to see their imperfections but that we must overcome.

Music changes everything instantly and I've learned to have it on constantly, happily

Use Sundays to review work done during the week, rest and stay unique.

I laid it out in whole hoping you could grasp the depth, breadth and urgency to act.

I've been down this path before/you remind me of someone I used to know and I declare: I don't want to know more.

TACOS FOREVER

Put all prior kitchen appurtenances in the basement and keep just one pan for tacos.

It's a pleasure to eliminate 80% of kitchen clutter. Put it all away then penuriously select back simpler.

Tacos with a little cheese and zucchini slice cooking in it. Fill with diced tomato, white onion, lettuce. Eat 3, now fast to tomorrow lunch.

RECAP

Emotional cut-off dissolves symptoms and sick systems maintain them.

The depraved are compelled because God gave them up.

All that sinning was just preparatory stage to finally tell the world.

The best saints were the worst sinners. I say "were" cuz now we're winners.

100 KAREN KELLOCK BOOKS

AFFINITY OR MISERY
AGELESS CORNUCOPIA
AMERICA AWAKE!
AMERICA'S DAFT ERA
ARTS OF PALEO FASTING
AUTOPHAGY ON CHEATERS
BACKSTABBING NEUROTICS
BETRAYAL TRAUMA
BOOMERS AND BROKENNESS
BOOT ON NECK
CHAMPION GUIDES
COMMIE NUTHOUSE
COMMIES
COMMUNIST SPIRIT
CONTAGION OF MADNESS
CONTAGIOUS MADNESS
CULTURE CLASH BASHED
DAFT LEFT
DAILY FASTARIAN
DAM RATS
DIVERSITY IS CRUELTY
E-RACE WHITE
EVIL FREAKS (Beyond Gross)
THE END OR A BEND?
FEMALE BULLIES AND FEMI-NAZIS
FEMALE CARNALITY
FEMALE DUMB DOWN
FEMALE POWER DRIVE
FEMINISM AND RUIN 1 & 2
FIX FOR MISFITS
FOOLS & TRAMPS
FREEDOM SPEAKING
FRENEMY ENABLER
FRENEMY LIAR
FRENEMY THIEF
FRENEMY TRAITOR
TRENEMY TYRANT
GENIUS IS HELD DOWN
GLOBALISLAM
GOD USES THE FLAWED
HAZE OF THE LATTER DAYS

THE HERD IN WORDS
HIX POLITIX
HOW THEY RUINED US
JUST SKIP DINNER
LE FEMME AND THE COMMUNIST SPIRIT
LIBERAL CHAOS & ROT
LIBERAL DOUBLETHINK
LIBERAL GALL 1 & 2
LIBERAL SHOVE-DOWNS
LOCK YOUR GATE
LOSERS and Femme Fatales
MANUAL FOR SUPERIOR MEN
MODERN ART FROM HELL
MOSTLY FAKE
NOTES TO CHAMPS 1 & 2
OVERCOME FRENEMIES
PC MAKES US CRAZY
PEOPLE ARE CRUEL
PEOPLE PROBLEMS 1 & 2
PERSECUTED GENIUIS
POLI-PSYCH MYSTERIES
PRETENTIOUS SLOBS
QUEEN BEE
RED NEW DEAL
RETURNING TO FIRST NATURE
SEASON OF TREASON
SEPARATE MEANS HOLY
SOCIAL HYPNOTISM
SOLITUDE SOLUTION
SUPERCILIOUS
THE SCHOOLS SCREWED EM UP
TOAD TO PRINCE
TRIALS CYCLES
TRUMP VS. GROUP
TRUST IN TRASH
THE TRUTH ABOUT PEOPLE
UNDERHEANDEDLY CLEVER
WALK TALL WITHIN WALLS
WE'RE NOT ALL ONE
WINNERS SKIP DINNER
WORK OR SMERK

KAREN KELLOCK PH.D.

M.S. Political Science, San Diego State. Ph.D. in Psychology, University of California Irvine. Postdoctoral: UCI School of Medicine, Dept. of Psychiatry [NIMH Grants]. Developed the Debris Theory of Disease, a theory of system pathology in 120 books and 22 textbooks for the general public. The theory has a general formula: All disease is obstruction, all recovery is elimination, all success is attraction. The three obstructions are people, habit and food. Remove obstruction and snap to your goals, waiting in the wings.

www.ingramcontent.com/pod-product-compliance
Lightning Source LLC
Chambersburg PA
CBHW061715250726
48657CB00002B/624